Surgeon in the Crimea

George Lawson

Surgeon in the Crimea

THE EXPERIENCES OF GEORGE LAWSON
RECORDED IN LETTERS TO HIS FAMILY
1854–1855

Edited, enlarged and explained by

VICTOR BONHAM-CARTER

assisted by
MONICA LAWSON
granddaughter of George Lawson

Constable London

First published in 1968
by Constable & Co Ltd
10 Orange Street London WC2
TEXT: Copyright © 1968 by
Victor Bonham-Carter & Monica Lawson
GEORGE LAWSON'S LETTERS:
Copyright © 1968 by Monica Lawson
All rights reserved
Printed in Great Britain
by The Anchor Press Ltd, Tiptree, Essex
SBN 09456090 0

TO

MAJ.-GEN. R. E. BARNSLEY

CB, MC, MA, MB, B.CH

CURATOR

ROYAL ARMY MEDICAL CORPS HISTORICAL MUSEUM

Contents

Illustrations

Preface

A very great deal has been written about the Crimean
War of 1854–6, and there are comprehensive collections of
official and private papers which may be consulted. The
Crimea is well documented and thoroughly condemned. A
deep impression of muddle, misery and disaster has overlaid
all else in the public mind: deriving principally from
William Howard Russell's letters to *The Times*, and from
the work of Florence Nightingale so brilliantly described
by Cecil Woodham-Smith.

For a long time this was my total impression too, since
for family reasons—in addition to everything else—I was
brought up on Florence. My grandfather, Harry Bonham-
Carter, was her first cousin, and he devoted a large part of
his life to her service. For forty-three years he acted as
Secretary to the Training School for Nurses at St Thomas's
Hospital, and his son Walter, my uncle, continued for another forty-three: 1861–1947. The School had been founded
by Florence and endowed with the proceeds of the Nightingale Fund—a sum of over £40,000 subscribed by the
public in recognition of her work in the Crimea—and
opened in June 1860 with fifteen probationers in residence.
It was not the first of its kind, but it gave enormous im-
petus to the progress of nursing as a serious and scientific
profession. There was every reason then why I should
venerate the name of Florence Nightingale to the exclusion
of everyone else, particularly in connection with the
Crimea.

It was not until Miss Monica Lawson showed me the
unpublished letters of her grandfather, George Lawson,

a young staff assistant-surgeon, who joined up just before
war broke out in March 1854, that I began to modify my
view. Not that Florence deserves any less glory than she has
received, but that the shadows cast by her name over others
have become darker and deeper than they ought to be—
too deep for truth. There is no doubt about the facts. The
Crimea was hell. But were the medical and supply services
so entirely to blame; and were Dr Andrew Smith, Head of
the Army Medical Department, Dr John Hall, his Principal
Medical Officer in the Crimea, and Mr William Filder, the
Commissary-General, the complete butchers and nincom-
poops that Florence made them out to be? It is easy to
think so now, because judgment by hindsight is a safe and
satisfactory exercise; and because medical and other
matters have undergone such revolutionary changes in the
last hundred years that nowadays Crimean attitudes seem
unbelievably ignorant, prejudiced and crude—and not only
in medicine. Even Florence, it is said, never admitted the
existence of germs, and she died in 1910!

To achieve perspective it is essential to search for the
causes of mistakes, beyond mere personal errors. What was
the state of medical skill in the 1850s? Why was the Commissariat so hidebound? Why were there no ambulances
and hospital ships worthy of the name in that fearful winter
of 1854–5? To try to answer such questions is to explain,
not to justify, many of the Crimean disasters—and to
understand the actions of those in authority, who have
been castigated wholesale in history.

This is a short book and by no means an exhaustive one.
The purpose is to tell the tale, not in terms of tactics and
battles, but of the experiences and observations of a young
medico, fresh to his profession and 'full of surgical ardour'.
Research has been confined to illuminating the references
in the text and to filling in the background, and has not
been conducted as an end in itself. It is thus a commentary,

not a thesis: guided and provoked by George Lawson's
remarkably cheerful, totally unaffected, letters to his family
at Forest Hill, then 'pleasantly situated between the village
of Lewisham . . . and Sydenham with its fine mansions'.

I am indebted to the following for assistance:

Miss Monica Lawson, to whom the letters belong, and
who has been tireless in seeking information, securing books
and papers, offering ideas, and conducting research on her
own.

Major-General K. F. Stephens, OBE, QHS, Commandant
of the Royal Army Medical College, Millbank, for permission to consult the archives of the College; and particularly
Mr M. Davies, the Librarian, without whose help the work
could not have been carried on.

Mr J. W. Barber-Lomax, MA, B.VSC, Assistant Director,
and Mr J. K. Crellin, B.pharm, MPS, of the Wellcome Historical Medical Museum and Library; and Dr Kenneth
Keele, MD, FRCP, Medical Consultant to that institution.

Dr F. F. Cartwright, LRCP, MRCS, FFARCS, Consultant
Anaesthetist and Lecturer in the History of Medicine at
King's College Hospital; and his colleagues.

I wish also to thank Lieut.-General Sir Neil Cantlie, KBE,
CB, MC, FRCS, KHS, formerly Director-General of the Army
Medical Services; Major-General R. E. Barnsley, CB, MC,
MA, MB, B.CH, Curator of the Royal Army Medical Corps
Historical Museum—to whom this book is dedicated;
Mr W. Lefanu, MA, FSA, Librarian, Royal College of Sur-
geons; Mr D. W. King, OBE, Librarian, Ministry of Defence
(Central and Army); the Borough Librarian of Lewisham;
and all others who have helped with information and
suggestions.

I have, wherever possible, attributed information in the
Notes and Sources; and I wish to thank the authors and
publishers mentioned there for permission to make quotations; particularly Professor Percival R. Kirby, MA, D.LITT,

FRCM, FRAI, of the University of Witwatersrand, Johannesburg, biographer of Dr Andrew Smith.

Finally, I wish to emphasise that, throughout the book, I bear full responsibility for the text.

Summer 1968   VICTOR BONHAM-CARTER
                                           East Anstey
                                           North Devon

Note. There is one technical difficulty, small but knotty, viz. George Lawson's title. Early in his career, being as much a general practitioner as a surgeon, he was known as *Dr.* Later, when he specialised in ophthalmic and general surgery, he was addressed as *Mr.*

1 : The Lawsons

Near the river Alma
Crimea
Sept. 22nd 1854

My dear Fanny

We landed on the Crimea, I think, on the 14th of Sept, being allowed to bring with us nothing but what we could carry on our backs, viz. a great coat and blankets, and after marching in the evening about 2 miles to the place where we were to bivouac, we made ourselves as comfortable as we could for the night, without tents and having to sleep, of course, on the ground. Unfortunately there was no wood to be found to make large fires, no water to be had anywhere that we could find, and the night a pouring wet one. Notwithstanding all these little dis-agreeables, being exceedingly tired I slept thro' all, and woke in the morning wet to the skin, as did everyone else in the army. We soon dried ourselves before large fires, made from the wreck of a small vessel found on the beach, and after a bath in the sea I was as comfortable as I could be. . . .

So wrote Staff Assistant-Surgeon George Lawson to his sister. There was a family likeness in all his letters between 17th March 1854, when he left Woolwich as a young volunteer, and 18th July 1855, when, invalided and on the way home, he said simply:

I am still in a very feeble condition, and you will, I am sure, be sorry to hear that I have entirely lost the use of my legs, and in some degree that of my hands also, but as my bodily

1

health is so good and my appetite rather voracious, I think
that as I gain strength I shall recover the use of my limbs
again. . . .

Understatement was part of George's character. As a
middle-class Victorian, he did not say everything he felt
and thought, and he certainly did not say it to his family.
In the extreme this is a trait we attribute to the hypocrisy
of the age, but there is no need to attribute any such thing
to George Lawson. As a doctor he spent all his life in close
contact with realities, and as a Victorian doctor he reacted
less sensitively perhaps to pain, smells and dirt than we do.
Had he not done so, he would never have survived that
terrible first winter in the Crimea. His letters were resilient
and restrained; and it is unlikely that the Lawsons – in
common with most people at home – ever knew the full
story.

George's father, William Lawson, was a City wine merchant. In 1821, with George Trower his partner, he had
purchased the old-established firm of Robert Jones and
Mardall, trading at 39 St Mary-at-Hill, Eastcheap; and set
up home over the business when he married Ann Norton in
1822. No children were born for several years, and in 1829
his niece Mary Ann, an orphan, came to live with him. In
the following year the first child, William, arrived: succeeded by George in 1831, Edward in 1832, Frederick in
1834, Frances (Fanny) in 1835, and Ellen in 1836. About
1835 the family moved to No. 9 The Grove, Blackheath,
where George first attended school – possibly the New
Proprietary School, housed in a classical-style building and
known to offer a strictly classical education. Soon the
Lawsons moved again, this time to Forest Hill, although
precise details are not known. Letters were simply sent to
Lawson, Forest Hill, Kent. For the voting register, William
gave his London address.[1]

Originally known as 'The Forest' and now absorbed into the wilderness of south-east London, Forest Hill[2] was then emerging from the Kent countryside. 'Pleasantly situated between the village of Lewisham, with a branch of the Ravensbourne running along its main street, and Sydenham with its fine mansions', it was fast ripening for development. Agents' advertisements already had a familiar ring.

The salubrity of the air, the beauty of the surrounding scenery and its close proximity to London, render it a most desirable place of residence for merchants and men of business generally.

Desirability had its drawbacks, however, and complaints were not long in coming.

The first want that calls for attention is good drainage, for that is necessary to health, and we do not want cholera. Next we want light; the dark gloomy state of our roads renders them unsafe to life and property.

Drains or no, the population was proliferating and forcing London far beyond its historic boundaries. Prosperous traders and professional men – the new rich so bitterly assailed by William Cobbett[3] – were determined to acquire gentility by moving out of the City. The revolution in industry and agriculture was detonating a revolution in society, and the acceleration of transport and the development of Forest Hill were conditioned by the enclosure of open land. In 1809 a canal had been cut from New Cross to Croydon, the rise at Forest Hill requiring twenty-five locks. In 1836 the canal was bought up for £40,000 by the Croydon and London Railway Company, which filled in sections of the channel and laid rails along a large part of the course. It may have been this development – or the prospect of it – that determined the Lawsons' second move, for the train service was relatively frequent and remarkably quick. The

B

8.17 a.m. from Forest Hill arrived at London Bridge at
8.35 a.m., and then William had only to walk over the
bridge to be at his office a few minutes later: a matter of
half an hour from door to door. Today it would take little
less, but Forest Hill is no longer the desirable countrified
suburb it was then.

By 1850 the Lawson family was growing up and away.
William, the eldest son, was an undergraduate at Trinity
College, Cambridge, the preliminary to a career in the Law.
Edward was going into the family business, the interest in
which he eventually sold before retiring to live the life of a
country gentleman in Sussex. Frederick would enter the
Church. The girls were in their 'teens and looking forward
to marriage. Fanny – after throwing over a Mr Parkinson –
became Mrs John Henry Johnson in September 1855. Ellen,
however, remained a spinster all her life.

George had already started to train as a doctor.[4] From
1848 to 1851 he was a student in the Medical Department of
King's College, London, following a course that featured
physiology under Dr Robert Bentley Todd; anatomy (des-
scriptive and surgical) under Professor Richard Partridge
and his two assistants, William Bowman and John Simon;
surgery under Mr William Fergusson; chemistry under Dr
Miller; medicine under Dr George Budd; and midwifery
under Dr Farre. Other subjects included botany, chemical
manipulations, forensic medicine, and *materia medica* and
therapeutics.

Several of these instructors achieved eminence. Dr Todd
had already made his mark as a physician. It was largely
due to his efforts that King's College Hospital had been
founded 1839–40. He was also the author of the standard
work on physiology, and co-editor with Bowman of *The
Cyclopaedia of Anatomy and Physiology*. Bowman was
elected Fellow of the Royal Society at the age of twenty-
five, and practised surgery both at King's and Moorfields

Eye Hospital, where George Lawson was to become his assistant in 1862. Earlier Todd and Bowman had been associated in the founding of St John's House, the purpose being

> to improve the qualifications and raise the character of Nurses for the sick, by providing for them professional training together with moral and religious discipline under the care of a clergyman, aided by the influence and example of a Lady Superintendent and other resident Sisters.[5]

This was an Anglican sisterhood, controlling lay nurses, and the forerunner of Florence Nightingale's Training School at St Thomas's Hospital. It is of interest that St John's House sent several nurses to the Crimea, where they served under Florence. One of them, Elizabeth Woodward, looked after George Lawson when he contracted typhus in May 1855 and accompanied him back to England.

Richard Partridge was one of the original Fellows of the Royal College of Surgeons. In 1831 it had been he who had suspected foul play when the corpse of the fourteen-year-old Carlo Ferrari was offered to King's College for dissection for the sum of 12 guineas – a case that so stirred public feeling that it helped hasten the passing of the Anatomy Act, 1832. His second assistant, John Simon, became the first Medical Officer of Health to the City of London. His colleague, William Fergusson, was regarded as the 'greatest practical surgeon of his day'.

George Lawson was a model student, qualifying with the minimum of delay. He gained certificates of honour for physiology, comparative anatomy and midwifery, secured his MRCS in 1852, and was promptly appointed House Surgeon to Fergusson. In the following year he became House Physician and Accoucheur. These appointments were by no means automatic, being determined by examination, so that competition for the few vacancies was keen. There is little doubt that he displayed great promise in a profession that was standing on the threshold of modernity. It was an exciting time in which to start a medical career.

2 : The maze of medicine

1848, when George began his studies at King's, was a year of political upheaval all over Europe and the peak of Chartist agitation in England. Social conscience, expressed for example in the Christian Socialism expounded by Charles Kingsley and Frederick Denison Maurice (who lost his Chair at King's on account of his theological opinions), strove with the social degradation of industrialism. Yet the two streams were often confused. Reformers accepted the challenge of *laissez-faire*, though it was the consequences they were trying to cure; while industrialists eased their consciences by building schools and churches. On both sides there was much moral earnestness, an impulse that drove good and bad along together in the same harness.

Inevitably medicine was involved.[1] The problems of disease had assumed frightening proportions in the overcrowded towns and stimulated both scientific and moral enquiry. King's, for instance, had been founded in 1828 upon the fundamental principle 'that every system of general education for the youth of a Christian Community ought to comprise instruction in the Christian religion. . . .' Three years later the College established a Department of Medicine and Surgery, the curriculum to allow for religious studies, since medical students had the reputation (not quite lost today) of being rowdy, irreverent and uncontrolled. Dr Todd, first Dean of the Department, told the Archbishop of Canterbury that 'the design was to give to Medical Education a tone and character it did not previously possess'; and no scholarship was awarded unless the candidate had previously satisfied the examiners as to his

7

knowledge of the Old and New Testaments. The opening of
the Teaching Hospital at the beginning of 1840 took the
process of moral and medical education a step further; for
while it enabled King's students for the first time to receive
clinical instruction at their own hospital, it also attended
to a desperate public need.[2]

The first King's College Hospital was housed in the old
St Clement Danes Workhouse in Portugal Street, near
Lincoln's Inn Fields, and provided 120 beds. The district
was densely populated and abysmally poor, over 40,000
people packed into little more than a quarter of a square
mile, a complex of dark alley-ways and disgusting courts,
inhabited by a mixed company of paupers and common
criminals. Much of it was swept away later to become the
site of the Law Courts; meantime squalor and pollution
were synonymous, and epidemics a constant scare. In 1848
two small wards were opened in the Hospital, intended
primarily for the treatment of cholera. There had always
been 'summer cholera' in England, so-called because it was
at its worst in the warm weather, but the mortality was
relatively slight. 'Asiatic cholera', however, was a recent
arrival and a deadly scourge. In 1848 70,000 people died
of it. And there were other diseases hardly less lethal:
tuberculosis, for instance, which accounted for more than
25% of all hospital admissions in the nineteenth century.
As yet there was no cure for any of these afflictions,
although preventive measures were in sight.

The idea that health was a national concern, part of the
pursuit of happiness of the greatest number, belonged in
Britain to the Utilitarian philosophy of the late eighteenth
and early nineteenth centuries, and was associated particularly with the name of Jeremy Bentham. It was an
important aspect of the moral impulse for social improvement; but the practical pioneers were Thomas Southwood
Smith, a Unitarian minister and physician, and Edwin

Chadwick, a visionary propagandist. Both were sanitarians, so tireless in their activities that a Government department, the General Board of Health, was set up in 1848; and Medical Officers of Health appointed to the main cities – Liverpool first, then London, where John Simon (one of George's instructors) made his name.

The sanitarians – of whom Florence Nightingale was one – did not know what caused disease. They adhered to the theory that it arose from *miasma* or bad air generated spontaneously by areas of decay or dirt, such as marshes, middens and accumulations of filth. This encouraged them, on a false hypothesis, to take the right preventive action – and none too soon. Basic necessities, such as clean piped water and proper systems for the disposal of rubbish and the burial of the dead were still lacking. Many town houses still had cesspits beneath them; others relied on street privies. Underground sewers, where they existed, were badly built; and all discharged into the nearest river, still the main source of drinking water – such being the cause of the 1848 outbreak. The Thames stank so badly that as late as the 1850s it was said to upset the Members of Parliament working at Westminster. The streets smelled no better, even when paved, and the removal of horse manure at cartfuls per mile was a major employment.

It was the sanitary measures introduced by Florence Nightingale that saved the situation at Scutari in 1854–5 and substituted decency and order for administrative chaos. She not only had her way in hospital routine, but moved by logical steps into the wider world of welfare. Ably assisted by Monsieur Soyer, chef of the Reform Club, she overhauled cooking arrangements and diet, and followed this by securing soldiers' rest-rooms and by acting as a private banker for their savings. In short, she started a welfare revolution and worked for the rest of her long life to consolidate and extend her early achievements. Yet, as has been mentioned, she is said never to have acknowledged the existence of germs.

By the Crimean War, however, the real clue to the cause of disease was close to discovery. Whereas the conception of *miasma* established likely sources of infection, the development of disease was sometimes attributed to fermentation caused by particles of organic matter entering the human body, whether from 'bad air' or from contact with an infected person. In the latter case this contributed to the thinking that lay behind the isolation of lepers in the Middle Ages and the establishment of quarantine stations. Inhuman and burdensome as the practice was, it often proved effective in that it halted the spread of diseases transmitted by contact.

Yet no one identified microbes, although their existence was known long before the 1850s. The invention of practical microscopes in the seventeenth century had enabled van Leeuwenhoek to see and make drawings of certain 'animalcules' or bacteria as early as 1683; and he realised that these were present in numbers beyond calculation in the human body. Although his discoveries were subsequently confirmed by other medical investigators, and their relation to disease surmised, no positive progress in this direction was made for almost three centuries, and then by a side-route.

In 1857 Louis Pasteur developed the discovery made twenty years earlier by Theodor Schwann in the field of fermentation: to the effect that the process was due to the presence of a living organism, and not solely to chemical change, as averred by Justus von Liebig. We know now that both factors are involved. Bacteria manufacture 'ferments', which in turn cause fermentation; but Pasteur pursued and proved beyond doubt what was still hotly denied – namely, that micro-organisms were the primary cause; and he demonstrated the point in experiments connected with the souring of milk and the contamination of

wine and beer. It was, however, the English surgeon Joseph
Lister in the 1860s who grasped the implications of
Pasteur's work and first applied it to disease: in short, that
micro-organisms might be the cause of putrefaction as they
were of fermentation.

Not long before this date surgery had only been attempted
in the last resort – the patient enduring a dreadful period
of anticipation hardly less intense than the physical suffering of the operation itself. Even so, many superficial
operations were carried out – and some others too – and
considerable progress made, notably by the brothers John
and William Hunter in the latter half of the eighteenth
century. Medical experience of this kind contributed to a
general understanding of anatomy and – by means of dissection and the rational observation of symptoms before
death – to a greater grasp of physiology and pathology.
Nevertheless in 1844–5 the year's list of operations conducted by Robert Liston, the leading surgeon of his day,
amounted only to: 'Lithotomy, 5 cases; herniotomy, 4;
tumours excised, 22; amputations, 10; excision of joint, 1;
ligation of aneurism, 1; perineal section for lacerated
urethra, 1; operations for phimosis and fistula in ano, 2;
and several plastics'.[3] Other operations more or less
commonly practised were trephining, thoracotomy, the
reductions of fractures and dislocations, and a few connected
with venereal disease, obstetrics, and the eye, ear, nose and
throat.

In 1838 a complete set of instruments 'with the modern
improvements' issued to regimental hospitals comprised: 3
saws, 24 curved needles, 4 amputating knives, 1 catlin, 4
tenaculums, 3 forceps, 2 screw and 2 field tourniquets, 2
trephines, 1 lenticular, 6 scalpels, 6 catheters, 3 trocars, 3
probes, 2 bistouries, 4 reels of silk, and various dental
items.[4]

A surgeon, in short, was prepared to undertake a fair

amount of physical carpentry; yet, however skilled he
might be, his efforts were continually brought to nought.
Ignorance of antisepsis and the absence of anaesthesia
meant that the majority of operations incurred a high rate
of mortality, owing to infection of the wound and the effect
of shock. For this reason abdominal operations were only
very rarely undertaken. Patients that survived did so
thanks partly to their innate powers of resistance, and
partly to the speed at which the surgeon worked. A modern
historian has written:

These were the days in which hospital gangrene assumed
epidemic proportions, and sepsis was an inevitable sequence of
operations. Compound fractures were treated by amputation,
with a mortality of at least 25%, while the surgeon wore an old
bloodstained coat with a bunch of silk ligatures threaded
through one of the button-holes, ready for use. During the slow
process of healing, a zinc tray contained the 'laudable pus'
which dripped from the wound. The stench of the surgical wards,
perhaps the least of the evils, may be readily imagined.

Small wonder, then, that a considerable degree of heroism was
demanded from the unfortunate patient who, having endured
the tortures of operation without anaesthesia, was still obliged
to face the pains and dangers of a septic wound. As for the
surgeon, he required not only 'the eye of an eagle, the strength
of a giant, and the hand of a lady', but also a degree of dexterity
and agility with which few men are favoured.[5]

The introduction of anaesthetics, however, opened the
door to modern methods of surgery. In 1846 ether was first
used successfully both in the USA and in the UK; and a
year later in Edinburgh Sir James Young Simpson demonstrated the properties of chloroform. The advantages were
soon seen in the relief of pain, in the complete relaxation of
the patient, and in affording the surgeon more time for his
work. But there were disadvantages too. Methods of
application were relatively crude, and it took some time to

arrive at a satisfactory system of inhalation. For one reason or another, patients continued to die on the operating table, and some surgeons were naturally anxious about the effect of the new drugs. Dr John Hall, Principal Medical Officer to the British Army in the Crimea, was among those who entreated caution, and he has been castigated in history for saying: '. . . however barbarous it may appear, the smart of the knife is a powerful stimulant, and it is much better to hear a man bawl lustily than to see him sink silently into the grave'.[6]

He was proved wrong, of course, but he was not wrong to express doubt. He never objected to anaesthetics – as some did – on religious grounds, or thought that screaming was actually beneficial, or that an operation was such a serious affair that a patient ought to be conscious of what was being done to him.

The most serious disadvantage of anaesthesia was not realised at first, and arose from the fact that, thanks to its use, surgeons had become bold and were performing many more operations; and yet – though diminishing – the death-rate remained high. As explained, it was Lister who took the next step, in following up Pasteur's work on fermentation. Postulating that micro-organisms might also generate putrefaction in wounds, he experimented successfully with carbolic as an antiseptic agent in the operating theatre. It was the turning-point. From this and the improvements Lister later devised, concurrent with the progress of bacteriological research, sprang the whole principle of antisepsis – and the recognition at last that without a comprehensive routine of sterilisation the new horizon revealed by anaesthetics remained a mirage.

All this, however, lay ahead. When George Lawson qualified in 1852, medicine was still in the early stages of transition: with anaesthetics a doubtful innovation, antisepsis undreamed of, and sanitation a luxury. Advanced

thinking had not percolated throughout the rank and file
of the medical profession, and treatment was still an
amalgam of unquestioning tradition and scientific method.
The ordinary doctor – civilian or military – had a stetho-
scope and was prepared to lance boils, raise blisters, let
blood, apply leeches and fomentations, and prescribe a
variety of draughts, pills, powders and boluses, constituted
by a surprisingly wide range of drugs, though of limited
effect:[7] for example, opium for sedation and pain-killing;
senna, castor oil and Epsom salts for purging; ipecacuanha
to induce vomiting; chalk and opium for diarrhoea; digitalis
for heart trouble; quinine and antimony for reducing fever;
squills for coughs; and mercury for venereal diseases. To
fortify the patient, the doctor would recommend brandy,
port and beef-tea; to soothe him arrowroot and salep.

Such was the state of medicine when, early in 1854, Dr
George Lawson volunteered for service with the expeditionary force, sailing east to aid the Turks in their defensive
campaign against the Russians.

3 : The unnecessary war

Turkey had been at war with Russia since November 1853: the cause – as Oman puts it in his classic school history – being 'a trivial quarrel between Greek and Latin monks in Palestine. . . . When Russia used her power in favour of the Greeks, Emperor Napoleon, eager to assert the influence of France in the East, replied by supporting the Latins. Both threatened the unfortunate Sultan with their displeasure, and when he decided in favour of the Romanists, the Czar proceeded to strong measures of coercion.' In short, Russian expansionism was released against Turkey, whose empire was considered an anomaly in an age of other people's empires. Other countries, as Tsar Nicholas well knew, were interested in eastern Europe – Austria and Britain, as well as France – and he offered to buy them off with Turkish property. Neither the French Emperor nor the British Cabinet led by Lord Aberdeen wished to see the balance of power disturbed, and both advised the Sultan to stand firm. Diplomatic pressure, however, was not enough. War broke out, the Russian Navy dominated the Black Sea, and the Russian Army crossed the Danube into Bulgaria. Little by little, opinion hardened and, with Palmerston pushing at the Foreign Office, France and Britain were gradually drawn in. By the end of March 1854 both countries were formally involved, and the British nation found itself committed to a major conflict for the first time for nearly forty years. The timing could hardly have been less propitious. The war was unnecessary and the British Army unready.

The British expeditionary force – far smaller than the

15

French, ill trained and worse equipped – amounted to less
than 30,000 men, organised in five divisions (four infantry,
one cavalry, with artillery and engineers). Owing to imperial
commitments in India and other foreign stations, the force
was assembled with difficulty. Yet, as events proved, its
fighting quality was high. Many of the officers and men
were to display extraordinary courage and skill in conditions
of appalling adversity. The higher command, however, was
incompetent. The senior generals were old – Lord Raglan,
the Commander-in-Chief, was sixty-eight and a veteran of
the Peninsular War – and all were unused to handling large
formations in the field. The staffs were likewise inexperienced
and untrained. Most serious of all was the mismanagement
at home, for – as was soon discovered – the British Army
was administered not by one authority or department, but
by seven, all largely independent of each other.

The basic fault lay partly with Parliament and the nation
at large, which had allowed the Army to run down after
Waterloo and deprived it of resources thereafter; partly
with the Duke of Wellington, who kept such a tight hold
on military affairs between 1815 and his death in 1852 – and
was so revered for doing so – that the Army became
atrophied. But there was another fault, of long standing
and sound constitutional origin: that of divided control as
between the military and civil authorities; and this was
exhibited in all sorts of ways, social as well as administrative. When the Army was recruited after the Restora-
tion, great care was taken to prevent it becoming ever again
the instrument of dictatorship. Although the King was
allowed to command the troops, real power rested with
Parliament through the agency of finance. All credits had
to be agreed by annual legislation (the Mutiny Act), while
the services of supply and transport were placed in civilian
hands, subject to the Treasury, which appointed commissaries for the purpose.

The system worked after a fashion, but it did not make for efficiency and it actively encouraged peculation. Since everything a soldier needed, other than ordnance, was put out to contract, everyone took a cut, and it was regarded almost as a breach of discipline not to do so. When Sergeant-Major William Cobbett, in his priggish innocence, tried to show up the Quartermaster of the 54th Regiment in 1791, he was thwarted by authority and compelled to flee the country. Likewise there was plenty of scope for corruption when it came to hiring horses and carts for moving stores. It was only towards the end of the eighteenth century that the principle of divided control was broken, and then not finally. In 1794 was raised a military unit known as the Royal Waggoners (first entitled a Corps, then a Train), which survived until 1833. The Train became the Duke's main transport service in the Peninsula, where for the first time soldiers and civilians – thanks to sheer necessity and Wellington's iron will – combined effectively together. Commissaries themselves did the work formerly done by contractors, set up their own depots, supplemented the military transport, and even organised the local construction of carts. Moreover, payment was prompt. Another good thing was done by the Commissary-General, who improved his men's salaries and introduced a measure of training. But it could not last. Once Waterloo had been won, old habits reasserted themselves. The Train was axed, and the Commissariat (responsible for all non-warlike stores) deteriorated into a department of accountants, putting everything out to civilian contractors as in the past. A few commissaries were allowed to keep their jobs in the field – on stations abroad and in Ireland, where William Filder was discovered and dug out at the age of sixty-eight, and promoted to the thankless post of Commissary-General in the Crimea. His story has often been told, for he was cursed during the campaign and vilified in history afterwards. Everything was blamed on him – the mishandling of contracts, lack of transport, non-arrival of stores, shortage of food and forage, red tape at base: all and everything. It *was* a frightful mess, and Mr Filder was an old man, past his best, without sufficient or trained staff, badly served at home. But the situation was such that no man alone, however clever and energetic, could have mastered it. The Crimean tragedy was the price paid for years of neglect, and Mr Filder's lot was aggravated throughout by the social stigma attaching to his civilian status – yet another legacy from the past.

Put succinctly, the Army was still divided into 'Teeth and Tail'.[1] The Teeth were the fighting men, the real soldiers, led at the top by elderly aristocrats all over sixty except the Duke of Cambridge, who was sent home prematurely; and lower down by far too many officers who looked upon Army service, with its three parades a week, as an agreeable way of passing the time before inheriting their estates. Although the gunners and the engineers (the scientific corps) were exempt, the cavalrymen and infantrymen (the purchase corps) had bought their commissions. And since purchase usually involved the possession of private income – one of the marks of a gentleman – it was only gentlemen who were regarded as fit to hold commissions. And they certainly did not concern themselves with the domestic chores of the Army, which were largely run by the Tail – commissaries and others, officially classed as civilians, including doctors.

It is known that in the seventeenth century, when British military history really began, each regiment had its own surgeon who – subject to confirmation by higher authority – owed his appointment to the colonel.[2] In many cases the surgeon purchased a commission as well in order to improve his military standing. Even so he was never able to exercise the privileges which attached to it, and he had to call on a military officer if he wished his orders to be carried out by any rank other than a medical one. In his own sphere, however, he reigned supreme, provided his own instruments, purchased medicines, and was subject only in a shadowy way to a very distant superior, the Surgeon-General. His assistant was known as the surgeon's mate, medically no better often than an apprentice, and who was otherwise in an ambiguous position, for as a warrant officer he was amenable to regimental discipline. At the end of the eighteenth century pay and status of both these men improved: the surgeon becoming the equivalent of a captain, the mate a subaltern; but the power to purchase regimental medicines was withdrawn. Another functionary, the staff surgeon, served in a hospital, where also the occasional physician might be found; but this was a superior being, a properly qualified doctor, appointed by the Physician-General or the President of the London College of Physicians.

An apothecary was originally no mere dispenser, but a senior doctor or surgeon, having charge of medicines and medical equipment (but not medical stores and comforts, the business of the purveyor). In time his status slipped and the rank was abolished, though reintroduced for the duration of the Crimea. For many years the Apothecary-General received 10% on all drugs purchased for the Army, a practice that provided Apothecary-General Garnier with a comfortable fortune, so that he had finally to be removed at the height of the Napoleonic Wars by Act of Parliament. The post then became a salaried one, and involved ordering all medical stores from the trade for issue half-yearly, after testing at the Army Elaboratory at St James's.

Finally, there was the purveyor, originally a doctor (as it was hoped that a man of his quality might be above peculation), but later a more lowly individual, although his job was important enough. The purveyor acted in effect as

c

commissariat officer to the hospital; supplying the beds, furniture and utensils; distributing the basic rations of bread, meat and rum; and providing the patients with medical comforts, such as cheese, chicken, vegetables, jellies, arrowroot, etc. He was also responsible for pay, burials, wills, admissions and discharges, and many other things, including hospital clothing and linen, which he issued to the matron. In war women accompanied the men, on the basis of 10% of unit strength, and – before the Crimea – worked in hospitals as a matter of course. A matron, usually a soldier's wife, was paid 2*s* 6*d* a day, but was concerned less with nursing than with washing the linen and cooking the comforts.[3] Hospital nursing was not properly performed by women until the advent of Florence Nightingale. All other work was done by male medical orderlies, who were not medically trained at all, but consisted of cast-offs from military units – their commanding officers being only too thankful to be rid of them.

No army medical service proper existed before the nineteenth century for the organisation of hospitals and the co-ordination of medical duties as a whole. Large hospitals were attached to garrisons, and small ones to regiments, but it was William III who introduced 'flying' or 'marching' hospitals for use in war (forerunners of field ambulance units): the wounded, after treatment, being passed back to 'fixed' hospitals at base. These field hospitals disappeared, however, after Marlborough's campaigns in the early 1700s. In 1756 an Army Medical Board was set up to control all medical business, but it soon collapsed through quarrels and was not replaced until 1810 – and then by a Department with a Director-General. This was the real beginning, since it coincided with the rise of a remarkable man, Sir James McGrigor, who 'made' the service.

McGrigor was Wellington's principal medical officer in Spain. He started badly, incurring the Duke's wrath after the Battle of Salamanca, when, *contrary to orders*, he arranged for the commissariat waggons to go forward and clear the battlefield. But the Duke soon recognised McGrigor's worth and encouraged him to repeat the experiment. It paid handsome dividends. 'In close co-operation with the staff he organised a scheme for evacuating the wounded, brought out pre-fabricated hospitals from home, devised a system of registration of casualties which is the basis of statistical returns today, and found a party of a thousand or more perfectly healthy "convalescents" sunning themselves in a kind of Butlin's holiday camp at Lisbon, and packed them off to their units.'[2(b)]

McGrigor held the post of Director-General from 1815 to 1851, and remained the Duke's right-hand man all through, holding the medical service together as best he could during this long period of Army neglect. Although he wore uniform and held His Majesty's commission, he was never able to integrate doctors and soldiers. 'He had no military rank and was always officially known as Dr McGrigor; and it is significant that in his despatch the Duke referred to him as "one of the most industrious, able and successful *public servants* I have ever met with".'[2(b)] Remarkably, Napoleon was just as well served by – and he thought no less well of – his principal medical officer, Larrey, who 'made' the French medical service, and personally designed the first practical ambulance waggon, the *ambulance volante*.

McGrigor was succeeded by Dr Andrew Smith,[4] who had been his assistant for the previous five years. Smith had joined the service in 1812 and spent fifteen years in South Africa, where he displayed remarkable scientific as well as medical ability, as a naturalist, anthropologist and explorer, living hard in what amounted to campaign conditions in a raw, developing and semi-lawless country. No one could accuse him of being an office doctor. Recalled to England in

1837, he rose rapidly in the Army Medical Department and
after 1845 worked directly under McGrigor. When the latter
was allowed to retire at last, he recommended Smith as his
successor. The authorities accepted the recommendation,
but decided that the office of Director-General was over-
paid and unwarranted in peacetime. They therefore
nominated Smith Inspector-General of Hospitals and
Superintendent of the Department at a salary of £1,200 per
annum, or about half the amount that had been paid to
McGrigor.

The Department was still ludicrously small, having a
staff of two assistants and six clerks. Moreover, the work
expanded at once, for it was decided to combine the two
medical services attached to the Army – the Army Medical
Department under Smith at 12 St James's Place, and the
Ordnance Medical Department under the Marquis of
Anglesey at 63 Pall Mall. 'The anomaly of having two
separately controlled medical establishments soon became
apparent to Smith, especially since the Ordnance Medical
Department was presided over by a nobleman who, although a distinguished soldier, was not a medical man at all'.
Accordingly on 25th February 1853 Smith was appointed
Director-General of the Army and Ordnance Medical
Department, retaining the office at St James's Place. Thus
the title was restored and the work doubled, but the salary
remained the same. The reform was, of course, long overdue,
but, taking place only twelve months before the outbreak
of war, it added unnecessarily to Smith's burdens, when he
was being overloaded with the problems of the Crimean
campaign.

Now that the Duke was dead, other Army reforms were
being planned, though all came too late for the Crimea. A
semblance of combined training was tried out with brigade
manœuvres at Chobham in 1852, a 'sham fight' that ended
in chaos, a lesson in itself that was never learned: namely,

that the senior commanders and their staffs were incapable of handling large bodies of troops in the field. A permanent camp was about to be installed at Aldershot, soon to become the principal training centre of the British Army. It had many advantages. It was close to London, and large enough to accommodate a considerable number of troops of all arms – a division at least – and there was some scope for exercises in the country round. Above all, it would concentrate in one place many of the aids and institutions needed to teach the soldier his profession – schools, workshops and ranges – and to keep him in good heart. But all this lay in the future.

Meanwhile, the Russo-Turkish War had started, and during the winter of 1853–4 the many independent authorities concerned with the British Army were unnaturally busy at their desks: the Secretary of State for War, who was responsible overall; the Secretary at War, who looked after Army finance and administration; the Chancellor of the Exchequer, who controlled the Commissariat; the Home Secretary, who kept an eye on the militia and the yeomanry; the Commander-in-Chief, sitting in the Horse Guards, who commanded the military forces at home, though not abroad. The infantry and cavalry were his business, but not the artillery and engineers, nor the fortresses, nor the arms, nor warlike equipment and stores – which were all the responsibility of the Master-General of Ordnance, who practically commanded an army of his own; and finally there was the Board of General Officers, a venerable institution dating from 1714, which did little else but worry about the uniforms of the infantry and the cavalry.

Andrew Smith received his mobilisation orders on 10th February 1854, six weeks before the declaration of war by the British and French Governments. He recorded:

When it was determined, in 1854, that a Military Force should leave this country and proceed up the Mediterranean, to aid the Turks . . . I was required to immediately provide an adequate Medical Staff, and the amount of stores likely to be wanted for hospital purposes. If I had been given to understand when I received this intimation that the troops were to be employed on the duties which are usually exacted of soldiers in times of peace, I should have have had no difficulty in deciding what I ought to furnish, but the having been on the contrary led to expect that they would probably soon be engaged in the field, in conflict with an enemy, caused me both much consideration and anxiety, the more especially as neither myself nor the officers of the Department had, from personal experience, a knowledge of all that would probably be found necessary for the wants of sick and wounded during a European war.[5]

McGrigor had filed all his documents with the utmost care, but none proved to have any bearing on what was to follow – a common experience. Smith had to rely entirely on his own judgment and grapple with an unprecedented situation with totally inadequate resources. That too is a common experience. It followed that he had to become the whipping-boy when the great British public woke up to the medical muddles for which they indirectly had been responsible.

Smith lost no time in getting down to work. Within twenty-four hours he had ready a complete list of medicines and medical stores needed for six months' active service by the force of 10,000 men who were to be sent to Malta to act 'as an army of observation'. On 17th February he forwarded the return of hospital stores, and added a plea for waggons to convey the wounded. On 3rd March he submitted models designed by himself. One was a two-wheeled vehicle drawn by a pair of horses, to take badly wounded men lying prone in the centre, and slightly wounded sitting in front and rear and along the sides. There was also provision for an emergency operating table and for hospital chests lashed beneath. The other was a four-wheeler drawn by six mules. It was divided into two compartments, one having four berths for wounded on stretchers, the other taking men sitting back to back. Both vehicles were reproduced in *The Illustrated London News* (see facing p. 82). Smith asked that a prototype be built of each under his personal supervision. There the matter rested for a time, so that in June William Howard Russell, correspondent of *The Times*, complained that only local bullock carts were to be had in Bulgaria, where the troops were then assembling. When Smith's waggons did arrive, they were left behind at the quayside at Varna as the expeditionary force moved on to the Crimea, and so were not available for the Battle of the Alma on 20th September. Later they came in for technical criticism, largely because there had been no time for trials before the campaign started.

Unfortunately it was found that the two-wheeled carts frequently upset on rough ground, and that the weight on the shaft was too great for the horses. The four-wheeled waggons were more satisfactory, but they proved to be too heavy for cross-country work, and at first there were no metalled roads. The excessive weight was due to the fact that they were, contrary to Smith's ideas, fitted with gun-carriage wheels, the War Office having refused to adopt them unless this was done, affirming that the Doctor's lighter type would not stand up to the work. As a matter of fact it was found necessary in the field to make use of other and lighter vehicles, such as the 'Irish cars' which had been constructed in Clonmel by the enterprising Charles Bianconi, mule chairs (as used by the French), and the like.[6]

Later an investigating committee found 'that while the stretchers used on Smith's waggons were admirable, many men "objected to be packed away in the catacomb-fashion on which the waggons are constructed". But they raised a

much more serious objection, namely that there were at the
seat of war no wheelwrights, saddlers, harnessmakers or
farriers, and "not a man who knew how to put the waggons
together when they arrived".'

Smith also anticipated the need for a corps of stretcher-
bearers. In the past drummers and bandsmen had done this
work, but they were neither trained nor sufficient in
numbers. Smith proposed the employment of at least 800
natives under military discipline, and arranged for his
representative, Dr Brett, who had lived in Turkey and knew
the language and conditions, to investigate. But the military
authorities on the spot pooh-poohed the idea, and Dr Brett
returned defeated. Ultimately a corps was raised independently by the War Office – called the Hospital
Conveyance Corps[7] – under Colonel Alexander Tulloch, a
military officer. It was a ludicrous failure, for the men were
all pensioners and drunks, and could hardly carry themselves, let alone wounded men. Furthermore, when they
arrived at Varna in July they were promptly decimated by
cholera.

These were but a few of Smith's troubles. Behind everything lay the fact that his powers were strictly limited and
he had to rely on a multiplicity of other departments to get
things done. Kinglake, author of the classic nine-volume
history, *The Invasion of the Crimea*, wrote:

If the Director-General of the Army Medical Department
wished to furnish to our hospitals in the East some kinds of
supplies, as, for instance, wine, sago, arrowroot, he had to send
his purpose revolving in an orrery of official bodies: for first, he
well knew, he must move the Horse Guards, and the Horse
Guards must move the Ordnance, and the Ordnance must set
going the Admiralty, and the Admiralty must give orders to the
Victualling Office, and the Victualling Office must concert
measures with the Transport Office, and the Transport Office
(having only three transports) must appeal to the private ship-

owners, in the hope that sooner or later they would furnish the sea-carriage needed; so that then the original requisition becoming at last disentangled, might emerge after all from the labyrinth, and – resulting in a actual, visible shipment of wine, sago, arrowroot – begin to receive fulfilment.

Shortly after issuing his initial orders, Smith was casually informed by Lord Raglan, the Commander-in-Chief, that the original force of 10,000 was going to be trebled and be sent on to Turkey. This involved obvious complications, and some less obvious ones. Turkey, he suspected, was a source of serious disease, especially for northerners: there would be cholera, typhus and other fevers, and malignant dysentery. The facts should be established at once, *before* the soldiers arrived; and permission was granted to dispatch three Scots surgeons to make a report. One of them, Dr Dumbreck, duly confirmed Smith's worst fears about the fevers; and he added that the winter climate in Turkey and the Danubian provinces was so severe that extra clothing, bedding and food should be provided at all costs.

Smith accepted this warning without reserve and wrote an urgent letter dated 13th April to the Military Secretary at the Horse Guards, describing the dangers. He also made specific recommendations: replace the tight red coat with a loose-fitting garment, waterproofed if possible, and belted to the body; substitute some practical headgear for the bearskin; get rid of the stiff leather stock worn round the throat; and issue each man with extra flannel shirts, underclothing and worsted stockings. He also appealed for bedding. The reply was negative; but a further report from Dumbreck prompted him to try again, and on 18th August he was assured by the Duke of Newcastle, Secretary of State for War, that at least the additional bedding would be forthcoming. As things turned out, it never reached the Crimea in time.

Smith also complained of the bad ventilation of army

tents, and recommended the immediate dispatch of 40,000 cholera-belts, a device that had proved useful in the epidemic of 1853. Finally, he expressed anxiety about the transport system. He wanted specially fitted hospital ships allocated to the Medical Department, and convalescent hospitals established in the Black Sea or the Aegean. This request had some effect, though belated, but Smith gained small credit for his foresight.

As 1854 proceeded, so the burden of anxieties and tasks grew heavier at 12 St James's Place. Smith made no attempt to build a personal empire, but merely upgraded two of his assistants and secured a slight increase in the salaries of his clerks, who were very badly paid. Without him – under the weight of work and the hurricane of abuse that was to follow – the Army Medical Department would have collapsed. He took steps, however, by careful filing 'to determine that my successor should . . . never have to encounter the many difficulties and perplexities which had fallen to my share'.[8] This proved invaluable when he had to give evidence before the commissions of enquiry, and enabled him to publish an official account of the medical aspects of the Crimean campaign. Facts were sacred – there was no lack of free comment.

4 : Off to the unnecessary war

LETTERS: 17th MARCH – 6th APRIL 1854

In the ordinary way it was no easy matter to join the Army as a doctor or surgeon. The Army Medical Service was not a purchase corps; and – as explained – those medical officers who had bought their commissions (such as Sir James McGrigor) had only done so in order to improve their military status. It was impossible to evade the requirement for medical qualifications, and these were considerable. According to the Regulations of 1840, repeated in substance in 1853–4, a candidate had to produce the diploma of the Colleges of Surgeons of London, Edinburgh or Dublin, and a long list of testimonials, which included eighteen months' service at a recognised hospital and varying periods of study of most medical subjects. He also had to have a university arts degree, a baptismal certificate, affidavits of moral conduct and character, and be unmarried, between the ages of twenty-one and twenty-five.[1]

Much of this went by the board after war was declared. The formalities for ordinary applicants were simplified and, for the first time in Army history, medical students were given emergency commissions. William Cattell, surgeon to the 5th Dragoon Guards, related his experience:

Whilst working for the M.B. (Bachelor of Medicine) at King's College, an old chum told me that he had been offered an Assistant-Surgeoncy in the Guards, which he could not accept,

and advised me to offer myself. . . . I had only to call at the
Army Medical Office and volunteer, which I did, and put my
name down for an interview. My reception was not cordial.
The Director-General, a Scotchman, in indifferent health and
careworn, with his hand on his liver, curtly demanded, 'and
who are you to think we need your services?' . . . Coming home
much hurt I could not conceal my discomfiture, and my people
communicated with Mrs Sidney Herbert, the wife of the War
Minister, who next morning herself went to see the potentate,
and I was summoned for examination. There were some thirty
groups of questions. At one o'clock Pilleau, who superintended,
came and watched me for a moment, then left the room; and
when I came home after 5, I was astonished to hear that Mrs
Herbert – soon after one o'clock – had brought news of my
having passed.[2]

Dr Andrew Smith – if he was in fact the potentate
referred to – must have had an off-day.

Douglas Arthur Reid, assistant-surgeon to the 90th Light
Infantry, had a different complaint. His first post was at
the Ordnance Hospital, Woolwich.

Although liable to be told at any time that my services would
be no longer required, the appointment being only a temporary
one, I was compelled to incur the expense of a Medical Staff
uniform and outfit, comprising the following items: Full Dress
– scarlet coatee with scarlet facings, gold epaulettes, cocked hat
with a black cock's feather, trousers with scarlet stripe. Undress
– blue single-breasted frock coat, tight at the waist, gold 'scales'
on the shoulders; forage cap, sword with black belt, mess jacket
with gold shoulder cords, military cloak, boots, gloves and
stock. . . . In less than six weeks afterwards, without receiving
any communication from the War Office, I was surprised to
find myself gazetted to an Assistant Surgeoncy in the 90th Light
Infantry then in the Crimea. At the same time an order reached
me to prepare for embarkation at an early date. Just then Army
uniforms were in a transition state. Nothing that I had provided
myself with as an Acting Assistant Surgeon on the Staff could

be adapted to the position of an assistant surgeon in a regiment, except the cloak, cocked hat, trousers, sword and boots. I had, therefore, immediately to procure a second outfit . . . also camp equipment, portable bed and bedding, bullock trunks, waterproof rug, canteen, supply of warm clothing and a Dean and Adams revolver. . . . The bill for all this a heavy one, and my pay was only 7s 6d a day. It took quite a year's pay to clear me of debt.[3]

George Lawson joined up some time early in 1854, before the declaration of war, and was immediately posted overseas. He sailed from Woolwich on 10th March in the *Cape of Good Hope*, of which there is very scant record. It seems, however, that she was relatively new, a screw brig, sail and steam, of 500 tons gross.[4] She took seventeen days to reach Malta. During this time George wrote several letters to his parents, posting them all together after arrival at Valletta. The voyage had been rough as far as the Bay of Biscay, when the weather improved and George got his sea-legs. The ship was then sailing 'at about 9 miles an hour'.

We number 9 surgeons, 4 engineering officers and one other gentleman, who is going out to volunteer his services to the Turks. You thus see that all our company is of the male sex, and a very excellent good-tempered set of fellows they all seem, everyone willing to oblige and lend a thing to another. The chief amusement of a part of the passengers is whist, which they commence in the morning, and do not cease playing until they go to bed. . . . We breakfast every morning pretty punctually at ½ past 8. . . . The tables are well covered, we have eggs and bacon, rump steak, pigeons, duck, cold hashed meat, ham, and in fact everything you can pile upon the table in the shape of eatables. At 12 o'clock is grog time; spirits and wine and biscuits are set on the table, and at 4 o'clock we dine, a dinner quite equal to any which you could get at any hotel. . . . At 7 we have tea and at ½ past 8 grog again, and at 10 we all go to bed . . . to be ready to begin the same process again at ½ past 8 the following morning.

But there were other employments and entertainments:

I forgot to mention that we have on board 100 of the Sappers
and Miners. They are a most useful set of men, and I really do
not know what we should do without them. They pull at the
ropes and assist the sailors in every possible manner. . . . Many
of them sing very well, and some of them play on different brass
instruments, so that in the evening we have singing, a little
dancing among them, and some music, all of which is very
delightful in the magnificent moonlight evenings that we have
had.

On Sunday there was church parade. 'All the soldiers
were had up, Captain Gibbs read the prayers, the soldiers
singing the morning hymn and a psalm, accompanied by
the brass instruments; it really was a very pretty sight.'
Less pretty were the first signs of unpreparedness:

From the hurry in which we started, and the short time given
for the vessel to get fitted out, many things unfortunately were
left behind, and amongst the many was a filter. The result has
been that the tanks being either new, or else very dirty, all the
water we have to drink is very nearly the colour of sherry from
the rust off the iron, and when it gets shaken up from rough
weather it is quite thick like soup. We have however now got
nearly accustomed to it, and as in other respects it is perfectly
sound and the iron is merely a tonic, it is not of much consequence.

George arrived at Valletta on 27th March, put up at the
Minerva Hotel, 53 Strada Stretta, and went to the opera his
very first night. He thought Malta 'a very fine looking
place' and – like most of his observations – his comments
were accurate and discerning:

The whole island is a rock. Every street is a steep hill, with
the exception of one or two. Many of them have steps all the
way up, with houses on each side. The tradesmen carry on their
business in the front of their houses, and you see tailors, shoe-

makers, tinkers, etc., all sitting just in front of their doors working. The houses are very lofty, and built so as to be as cool as possible. The hotels are quadrangular, enclosing a square in the centre, somewhat like the hotels in Paris. Around each floor there is a covered balcony, and most of the rooms open out of this, so that you can always have your door open and, if it rains, you do not get the rain in your rooms. The houses are built of white stone, the rooms very large and high, and entirely destitute of any furniture, with the exception of a wooden table and chairs. I am only speaking of things as I find them. My hotel, although very comfortable, is not a very bright specimen.

George only stayed in Malta ten days. The place abounded with troops, mostly British,[5] who landed only to be trans-shipped for the next stage east. Time did not hang heavily. George busied himself searching for a servant, looking without enthusiasm at the ladies and observing local life.

Dogs here are abundant. They seem to claim no master, but wander about the streets. We have also another wanderer in these parts, he comes principally at night, I mean 'the little thing what hops'. For the first two nights I was somewhat disturbed by them, but now I am resigned and indifferent to their torments.

War was declared on the day of George's arrival, but the news had not reached Malta and rumours were rife.

We have today received glorious news from Constantinople, in that the Turks have again gained a glorious victory over the Russians, who have lost about 3,000 men. I am afraid it is too good to be true. . . . We are hourly expecting the *Banshee* which is expected to bring over Lord Raglan and Prince George [The Duke of Cambridge] and, it is said, an announcement that war is declared. I hope that such is the case. . . . When we arrived, the first news we heard was, at dinner on board, that the Emperor Nicholas had rejected the ultimatum – when immediately one of the officers got up and proposed the Emperor of

Russia's health, which was drunk by all. I think they would
have been sadly disappointed had they come out for nothing.

For Malta the war was an economic boon. Money poured
in, both now and later, when the island became a military
and convalescent base, and developments were already in
hand in the harbour, where a dry dock had been installed
in 1848. So large were the fortunes being made by the
Maltese that – according to one historian – smokers plugged
their pipes with golden sovereigns, and this whole period of
prosperity passed into common parlance.[6]

The 1850s saw the start of active British interest in
Malta, an interest without the arrogance that coloured the
later years of colonialism. It was particularly out of place
in Malta, which enjoyed racial homogeneity when Britain
was still an offshore island full of warring tribes. The
Maltese derive their origins and their Semitic language
from the Phoenicians arriving in the second millennium BC
and the Carthaginians who succeeded them. Their character
altered little under successive overlords – Romans, Arabs,
Sicilian Normans, and aristocrats of Anjou and Aragon, who
possessed the island by inheritance or by war during the
Middle Ages. In 1530 Malta was presented by the Emperor
Charles V to the Order of the Hospital of St John of
Jerusalem, lately expelled by the Turks from the island of
Rhodes. This Order was a legacy of the Crusades, and had
grown into 'a powerful and wealthy body of celibate nobles
vowed to the oddly associated tasks of tending the poor,
healing the sick, and waging what was in effect a perpetual
war on Islam in the Mediterranean'.[7] An international company, grouping its Knights on a basis of nationality into
eight Langues, the Order settled successfully into Malta
and survived an historic siege of four months by Sultan
Suleiman in 1565. Thereafter it created a cosmopolitan
culture of remarkable unity and magnificence until,

deteriorating into an anachronism, it fell – as Venice did – before the impatience of Napoleon.

The French seized and looted Malta on their way to Egypt. Some of the silver plate was melted into bullion to pay Bonaparte's troops, while other treasure was lost in the *L'Orient*, sunk in the Battle of the Nile. Much more might have found its way to France had not the Maltese risen against the invaders and – with Nelson's help – compelled the French to evacuate the island in September 1800. The British remained, reluctantly at first. The Knights were discredited and the Maltese did not want them back. Instead, they petitioned for incorporation in the British Empire, and it was principally on this issue that the Peace of Amiens collapsed, for possession of Malta decided the mastery of the Mediterranean.

In 1814 incorporation was agreed, and a year later confirmed at Vienna. Sir Thomas Maitland was appointed Governor and, until 1824, included within his domain the Ionian Islands as well as Malta and its dependency of Gozo. 'King Tom', as he was called, had arrived in Malta in 1813 when an outbreak of plague was decimating the population and trade was at a standstill. The island's treasury was empty and vigorous measures were needed to restore confidence. 'King Tom' – a strong man, given to strong action and strong language – did all this and much more, for it was he who really wrested Malta out of the Middle Ages. He separated the executive, legislature and judiciary, and gave the judges fixed salaries in place of fees from clients. He organised the administration, laid the foundations of education, revenue and public health, and got on well with the Roman Catholic Church, which then, as now, dominated the civil life of the island.

Maitland's work was carried on by a series of generally sympathetic Governors, helped by a handful of British and Maltese officials. In 1831 a Maltese, Francesco Saverio

D

Caruana, was appointed Archbishop; and the diocese was placed – at the request of the British Government – directly under the Vatican. Religious toleration of non-Catholics, however, came later, and with it the practical separation of Church and State, when all ministers of religion were debarred from the Council of Government. All this formed part of the aftermath of the 1848 revolutions in Europe, which helped liberalise the Maltese Constitution and speeded several boatloads of refugees towards the island, mostly Italians. Great sympathy was felt for Italy, for there was as yet no political issue affecting Malta. Italian was the language of the courts and the Church, English of commerce and administration, while Maltese – still to be codified and grammaticised – was regarded merely as the peasants' parlance.

Although the era of the Grand Tour was over, Malta was a welcome stopping-place for educated travellers, with its magnificent archaeological and architectural heritage, and pleasant climate and society. Samuel Taylor Coleridge was useful as private secretary to the Civil Commissioner in 1804–5 and said some nice things about his stay. Byron was offensive, arriving in 1809 to take Arabic lessons and fall in love with two ladies simultaneously. In the following year Lady Hester Stanhope paid a short, unremarkable visit, *en route* to adventure in the Middle East. Disraeli turned up in 1830, wore flamboyant apparel and conducted himself more or less outrageously. Next year poor old Walter Scott, broken in health, exhausted by the demands of his creditors, and written out, came to Valletta for three weeks. He was powerfully affected by the magic of Malta, and determined to write a story about the Siege. He started work, actually scribbled 85,000 words, but died at Abbotsford before he could finish it. It was not a good book. In 1844 W. M. Thackeray looked in on a P. & O. cruise, and composed five pages of meaty journalese for his travel book,

A Journey from Cornhill to Cairo. Finally, in 1848, Edward Lear paid the first of a series of visits, but he seemed rarely in good spirits. Neither the British nor the Maltese wanted his pictures.

Thus – Malta at the time of the Crimea. In circumstances other than those of war, George Lawson might well have stayed longer and enjoyed himself more thoroughly. As it was, after only ten days, he embarked on the *Kangaroo*[8] carrying 1,000 troops, destination Gallipoli. He was however 'never in better health or more jolly'.

5 : Gallipoli

Of all the uncivilised, uncultivated, miserable places you have ever seen or heard of, I should think Gallipoli would surpass all. They seem to be at least 3 centuries behind any place I have ever seen.

Such was George's first impression of the Turkish port of Gelibolu on the north side of the Dardanelles. He had little regard for the origins of this historic territory, the ancient Thracian Chersonese, a peninsula saturated with time, emerging as an Athenian colony under Militiades in the sixth century BC, lost and regained by Pericles in the fifth, and passing finally to Philip of Macedon in the fourth. It retained its Grecian character beneath all the subsequent conquerors of Thrace – even the Turks, who had been in possession for 500 years when George arrived on the morning of 13th April 1854.

The houses are all miserable wooden things, more like very old country barns with a few red tiles on the top. The streets are all on the incline, and in such a miserable condition that if they had but left them in their natural condition, without attempting to lay down stones, they would have looked much better and have been far more easy for walking. There is not a single horse or mule (with the exception of those brought by the English and French) in the place, and the beasts of burden are buffaloes and very small bullocks, which pull a sort of wooden cart at the rate

38

of about 2 miles an hour at the outside. You may imagine the size of the bullocks when I tell you that, when I went this morning to the Commissariat for my rations, I saw a man throw down a bullock by its horns, another man tied three of its legs together like a sheep, and they deliberately nearly cut its head off, the animal being able to offer little resistance.

There is a large market place here, and the chief business seems to be carried on there. The Turks sit crossed legs on the counter, and smoke, and swindle in a shameful manner all the French and English, receiving their money and giving what change they think fit; in fact, I think, they will give nearly as much change for a penny as they do for a shilling. They do not seem to think anything about our coming here to fight for them, and do not render the slightest assistance for the embarkation of troops, or providing provisions etc for the Army.

The six Medical Staff (myself included) are quartered in what is considered one of the best sort of houses. It is very clean, with whitewashed walls, built very much like a large barn or stable, with three rooms above the ground floor which would answer very well for horses, if we had any. The structure of the house is so slight that the landlady requested that we should not bring up all our luggage, in case we should break the floor thro'. . . . We have no chairs or table, but a sort of broad platform about one foot from the ground, on which you are supposed to sit in Turkish fashion. The language spoken here is, for the most part, modern Greek, and a little boy yesterday showed us a book he was reading, and to our surprise we recognised our old school book *Xenophon*. I wish I had a good Greek lexicon and I think I could get on pretty well. . . . When we unpacked our goods, the landlady called up her son to look at them, and turned over the jug and soap dish with the greatest amount of curiosity. I am sure, from her manner, that she had never seen anything of the sort before.

I think you will gain the best idea of the town by imagining that you took about 300 or 400 small lanes out of the most confined part of London, none of them larger than St. Mary-at-Hill, place them together at all angles, and build a lot of very miserable wooden houses, made so that they just touch each

other across the road, then turn up all the paving stones, and
you will have a pretty good idea of the town of Gallipoli. None
of the streets have any names, the result is that you have no
means of guiding yourself home again after you have left your
house, and I seldom go without losing my way. . . . I don't
think they know what paint is here, as I have not seen a single
painted thing. The General has his name written on his door with
a piece of chalk.

George accustomed himself quickly to the strange conditions and even came to enjoy them. His chief complaints
concerned relatively minor matters common to most campaigns – the infrequencies of mail from home, the high cost
of postage payable both ways, uninteresting food and the
lack of firm news about the war. He knew that the reason
for landing troops at Gallipoli was to provide a reserve
force in case the Russians broke through in the north, and
to fortify the peninsula. This was the main task of the
British Engineers, detailed to cut a continuous trench
system at the narrow neck between the Gulf of Saros and
the Sea of Marmora, construct landing-places and repair
the vile roads – a herculean work. Otherwise, as the fighting
continued to favour the Turks, Gallipoli became more and
more a transit area, with troops passing forward to Adria-
nople, Scutari and Varna, or by-passing the territory
altogether. Rumours always abounded, and swung wildly
from one extreme to another: that the Russians were
advancing deep into Bulgaria, that Odessa had fallen to
the allied navies, even that Admiral Sir Charles Napier had
captured Cronstadt with a British squadron. The one
certain thing was the uncertainty of the climate and its ill
effects.

The nights have been most dreadfully cold; now however the
weather is improving, and I think we shall go to the other
extreme, as I am told Gallipoli is a very hot place. Owing partly
to the cold and partly to drink, we lost three of the 93rd High-

landers in one night. Two of them were brought home very drunk, in fact perfectly insensible, and placed in their tents. In the morning they were found dead and quite cold. Early the same morning the Chief Piper went out with a fatigue party and came home rather tipsy, and he in a few hours shared the same fate.

By early June the day temperature was exceeding 100 degrees Fahrenheit in the tents.

The soldiers now commence their drill at half past 3 in the morning. The Chaplain on Sunday performs service at 6 o'clock at one camp, and 7 at another; and even then it is so hot that many of the men are frequently obliged to fall out. An order has come out allowing the men to go about without their stocks. The officers go about town in a most dishabile style; straw hats and wideawakes are the fashion, with white trousers. . . . One feels inclined to do nothing but drink lemonade and eat ices which, you will be surprised to hear, we have in abundance, of course manufactured by the French.

George commented frequently on the French, sometimes to their detriment, more often not. The remarkable thing was that the two armies, though traditionally hostile, continued to get on very well together – despite the occasional fracas.

The French and English soldiers get drunk in the most disgraceful manner, but particularly the French. . . . Four nights since, about 10 o'clock, a number of Frenchmen (I think about 6 or 7) knocked at our door and asked for admittance. They were all tipsy and said they wanted wine. We of course told them they could not come in, that we were English officers and had no wine to give them. They did not however content themselves with this, and said they were Anglo-Francais, that they would come in, and if we did not open the door to them they would force it, and immediately began to put this threat into execution. We took but little notice until we heard them charge at the door with their short swords, and as the door is

anything but strong, we expected they would get in any minute.
So we loaded three pistols with the intention – if any of them
did succeed in getting in and showed the least violence – to
shoot him. Fortunately however in firing off a couple of caps, to
see if the nipples were clean, we frightened them, and shortly
after they disappeared.

George admired the French, principally for their pro-
fessionalism, their good and plentiful equipment, and the
ruthless way they dealt with the local inhabitants.

They understand doing things much better than we do. The
way in which they have provided for the soldiers is wonderful.
They seem to have thought of everything, they have even
brought machines for roasting the coffee and grinding it, as
you can only get it in a raw condition. They have taken some
of the best sheds, and are fitting them out as eating and drinking
shops; and now that a few small horses are being brought here
from the country, they are buying them all up; a veterinary
surgeon looks at them and, if moderately sound, buys them.
. . . The only way to deal with the Turks is as the French do.
They take what they like, and pay what they consider a proper
value. We are not allowed to do anything of the sort, and the
consequence is that we pay double for everything. . . . They
have now landed a great quantity of artillery, and are practising
at a target in the morning. They have an immense number of
horses and have brought forage for them, and commissariat
provisions for their troops – thus to a great extent rendering
themselves independent of the country. They are also much
quicker in their movements. They will, almost, land from their
transport vessels 2,000 men and have them encamped 2 miles
away, while we are looking for boats. Stationed off Gallipoli are
5 French frigates, but not one English. They have also a little
tug steamer to assist in landing their troops. The result is that
when a troop ship arrives, the men-of-war send their boats, and
the tug boat also assists, and in an incredibly short space of
time the men are landed.

The French understood the value of prestige in other

ways. William Howard Russell, correspondent of *The Times*,
related that when Lord Raglan, the British Commander-in-
Chief, arrived on 28th April, there was no one to meet him.[1]
The arrival of Prince Jerome Napoleon, cousin of the
Emperor, was celebrated somewhat differently – as George
described:

> The following day, the 29th, while sitting in our room, we
> were aroused by hearing a tremendous firing. At first we thought
> it must have been some Russian vessels endeavouring to sail
> past in false colours, but could scarcely imagine such a rash
> proceeding; so we hurried down to the beach to see what was
> the matter, and found that Prince Napoleon had just arrived,
> and the four or five French men-of-war lying off Gallipoli had
> been giving each a French Royal Salute, which consists of 101
> guns. As he was shortly going to land we remained to have a
> look at him, and as soon as he disembarked all the vessels gave
> him another salute. It was a very fine sight to see all the vessels
> firing. The Prince was met by all the French Generals and Staff,
> the two Paschas and a Turkish bodyguard. The English General
> met him at the house at which he was going to stay. . . . Last
> Sunday the French had a review of all their troops, and as it
> was expected to be rather a fine sight there was a large number
> of people to see it. We all had to turn out in full dress, cocked
> hats, and dress coats.

Russell impressed George favourably:

> I read in *The Times* newspaper which came out here a capital
> account of Gallipoli, headed from 'our correspondent'. He is a
> Mr Russell, an exceedingly amusing man, a general favourite
> out here. He remained at our quarters for some time, and would
> write his letters for *The Times* when the room was full of men
> and all talking. His account of Gallipoli is perfectly true and
> not in the least degree exaggerated. What astounded us most
> was the cool manner in which the Duke of Newcastle [Secretary
> of State for War] contradicts his statements and makes out that
> the arrangements out here are admirable.

Russell had reported adversely on the arrangements, 'or rather non-arrangements for the reception of our troops at Gallipoli'. He had complained particularly that the commissaries 'were not provided with interpreters or staff, that they were ignorant of the Turkish language, and that all their proceedings were necessarily slow and tedious'. This had been denied by the Duke in the House of Lords. George then quoted from his own experience:

For the use of the General Hospital at Gallipoli, a number of houses have been taken at different parts of the upper portion of the town, and we have at present about 70 men there. And how do you think the cooking arrangements are conducted? There is one man to act as cook for the whole. He is furnished with one camp kettle holding about 20 pints of water, he has no fireplace, but with a tripod to stand the kettle on and wood to make the fire, he manages to turn out something about the normal times for men to eat, and the fire is made upon the ground. . . . Two days ago a private met with a fall and broke his lower jaw in two places, and for want of proper splints I had to take the pasteboard covers of the *Wide, Wide World*, a little book which one of the men had out here, and with that the man had his jaw set. It is, I believe, perfectly true that the necessary things are on the road out here, and that many have gone on to Constantinople, but that is no comfort for the sufferers here.

The doctors, as always, were in constant demand:

The natives here are, I think, without medical men, as we are continually being applied to at all hours of the day to see some of them. . . . I saw a boy the other day in the street with a harelip. I accordingly decoyed him to the Hospital and operated on him, and as the case has turned out pretty favourably I have gained a great reputation among them. Yesterday I tapped an old Greek lady for dropsy – I trust that she will do well. My case of instruments, altho' some laughed at me for bringing them out, have turned out very useful. Another advantage is that one gets introduced into their houses, and are enabled to get a glance at the girls who would otherwise be almost entirely hidden from our view. They certainly have very pretty faces. . . .

George's desire to see more young female faces was gratified one day by a dramatic event:

Three days since, we were alarmed here by a fire. . . . The amount of confusion and noise can scarcely be imagined. The Turks and Greeks, miserable wretches, did not know what to do, but all in the immediate neighbourhood turned their clothes into the street, and the women and children commenced crying. A number of French and English Engineers soon arrived, and as the only way of stopping the fire was to pull down a number of houses, they set to work to do so. In a very short space of time a sufficient number of houses were knocked down on either side of the fire, and it was allowed to burn itself out. The Turks, after a while, certainly did bring up two little things which they called fire engines, but when I tell you that they were carried on men's shoulders, you may imagine of what size they must have been. . . . The way in which the fire is supposed to have taken place is this. During the last week there has been nothing but a series of feasts among the Greeks, and on Friday night in our house the landlady came up to light a lamp (which I suppose is a religious one) placed opposite some sacred pictures near the ceiling, and left it burning all night. Processions paraded the street about 3 or 4 o'clock in the morning, and every person nearly brought a lamb and killed it. What the meaning of all this is I cannot say, but probably one of these religious lamps set fire to the house. Now this fire revealed a mystery, for living here you would fancy that the whole population consisted of men and a few old women, but at the same time you wonder at seeing so many beautiful children about the streets. In the hurry of scrambling out of their houses, the young girls – who are always kept close at home – turned out, forgetting even to cover up their faces, as is usual with them. It really must have been a treat to the poor creatures to breathe a little fresh air, as during the whole time I have been here, I have hardly seen a single girl above 12 or under 40.

George, though fully convinced of his innate superiority
as an Englishman, could not resist a strong feeling of
fascination, even affection, for local life and customs – the
strict preservation of storks, the cocks that started crowing
long before dawn and answered each other all over Gallipoli,
the way the Turkish soldiers cheered the Sultan every
evening for having provided them with food, even the
fierce dogs that consumed the offal and set on him one day,[2]
or the shopkeepers who impudently addressed every
Englishman as 'Johnny'.

There are also a number of minarets placed in different parts
of the town, they are a sort of mosque, and the people do penance
at the top of them nearly every evening by making the most
miserable sort of noise, which I believe they call singing; but it
is difficult here to find out what they really are doing, as no one
understands the language excepting two or three Government
interpreters, and you are obliged to arrive at your own conclusions from what you see.

George was constantly bothered about servants – they
charged high prices and never stayed long – and since he
was not yet attached to a regiment, he had to find one for
himself. In Malta he had tried to persuade the Captain of
the *Cape of Good Hope* to part with a little boy he had on
board. 'He was such a jolly little fellow, but it was no go,
altho' I offered him £1 a month and his grub, which the
Government would find for him.' At Gallipoli at first he
was still without help, and he and his fellow doctors had to
act as cook and porters themselves.

Yesterday I had to carry some of my luggage on my shoulders
through the streets, and this morning I went down to get my
rations and brought them up myself. . . . The most disagreeable
part of doing for yourself is having to get your own meat and
bring it home, cleaning your own boots, and washing up the
dishes after you have finished feeding.

The authorities then relented.

Mainly through Col. Sullivan, Assistant Adjutant-General, we
have now been allowed two soldiers to act as our servants,
without interfering with our allowances, as he was disgusted at
seeing me carrying up meat and drawing water; and as we have
now picked up a Maltese servant who came out here on spec, we
are pretty comfortably off in the way of domestiques. I still
however accompany the man in the morning for our rations,
as I find that we get much better served when I go myself.

Rations were adequate, but dull, and so it was extremely
irksome to find that, when additional luxuries did arrive,
the right to buy at nominal prices – coffee at 6*d*, sugar at 2*d*
and tea at 1*s* per lb – was limited to regiments. Eventually
the matter was put right, but only after representations
had been made to Lord Raglan himself.

Horses were also hard to come by, and officers had to buy
their own, if they could be procured at all. George had
plans to purchase a mule, although these animals were
nominally issued by the Government to carry military
baggage and medical panniers. Eventually he succeeded
in buying two horses, one for pack, the other for riding.

The pack horse is a white one, very much in disposition like
our old friend at Ilfracombe, a beast that will always go altho'
I only paid £5 for him. I can trot him against any horse of his
size in Gallipoli, and he is one of the best for carrying a dead
weight. He does not stand much higher, if any, than Aunt's
pony, but he will carry 12 stone 20–25 miles easily. My other
brute is a vicious fellow, and keeps up a perpetual neighing like
the horses in Paris, so that I can be heard long before I am seen.
I would sell him if I could get his price. He can however stand a
good long day's work. The way in which they shoe them here is
to cut the foot quite flat, and cover it entirely – frog and all –
with a flat piece of iron rounded off to the shape of the foot and
having a hole in the centre. At first I strongly objected to this
mode and had my riding horse shod English fashion, but the

animal in a very short time went lame, and he is now obliged
to remain in the stable with his shoes off. As soon as he gets
well I shall have him shod Turkish fashion.

Local saddlery, however, was poor stuff and George had
to send for a consignment from England. By the time it
arrived he hoped to sell off his riding horse to an un-
suspecting Frenchman. 'I should not like to sell such a
disagreeable animal to an English officer.'

The monotony of life at Gallipoli was broken by a
welcome expedition across the straits to Abydos, where
there were plans to convert a large building into a hospital
capable of holding about 500 beds. He and another staff
surgeon were detailed to make a report, and left Gallipoli
on 9th June, in company with Major-General Sir Richard
England, commander of the 3rd Division, and Consul
Calvert and his wife. It was not a very serious inspection,
and George's strongest impression derived from the
Calverts' hospitality and their visit to the local Pasha,
the great man of the place.

At this present time it is the fast of Ramadan, and all the
Turks pass the day in bed. At sunset, when the cannon fires,
they get up, pray a good deal, eat and refresh themselves, and
return to bed again at a certain early hour in the morning when
the gun again fires, and there they remain till sunset, when they
go thro' the same process again. The poorer Turks are not able
thus to pass the day of fasting in bed, but they go about their
work as usual, but do not eat or drink during the day. . . . All
the business with the Pascha is transacted during the night.
When we arrived at the Pascha's house, which is a fine building
for the place, he was at prayers. We saw him kissing the ground
with his face towards the east, and performing those little
eccentricities which are the peculiarity of the Mahommedan
religion. We did not of course disturb him, but were shown into
a capacious room with well-padded cushions all round, to wait
until he had completed his devotions. In a short time he came

in and we had the honour of being formally introduced to him,
his three priests, the chief civil and criminal judges, and a few
others, and after being requested by him to take our seats, we
made ourselves easy on his cushions. In a few minutes four or
five pipe bearers came in, each bringing with him a long chabouk
or pipe already filled and lighted, and going down on one knee
they each presented us with a pipe, placing the bowl in a silver
dish to prevent the ashes being dropped on the floor. The
mouthpieces of the pipes were very handsome, they were composed of an immense piece of clouded amber with a ring of
diamonds around them. Coffee, very strong and sweet, but at
the same time very good, was presented to us in a similar
manner, the cups were not bigger than egg cups, made of china
and set in silver. The pipes being finished we were instantly
furnished with fresh ones. Lemonade made with rosewater was
then brought in, and after remaining for about an hour, as he
was being called to prayers, we wished him good night and
retired.

George wrote regularly to his family – addressing parents,
brothers, sisters, and his cousin Mary in turn. All his letters
were laced with hunger for home and a longing for every
scrap of news, however trivial. His father had cut down his
smoking to ease a cough, and George sent him a consignment of cigars and three boxes of cigarettes, 'nothing more
than a little Turkish tobacco rolled up in a piece of tissue
paper, and covered over with a tobacco leaf. They are only
4s 2d per hundred.' He remembered birthdays, or tried to,
and told Fanny how much he valued the daguerreotypes.
'Sometimes, after I have been looking at them and I need
hardly say admiring them, I ask another man his opinion,
and you are always recognised as my sister.'

The consecration of the new church at Forest Hill stirred
him to write:

Sunday here is rather a dead day, there are no churches and
all the shops are shut; but as the shops are frequently shut for

every slight occasion, one has difficulty to remember the days
of the week, and I frequently get quite out of reckoning. We
have not even anyone to sing 'Train up a child', which always
used to mark the Sunday evening at Forest Hill; and tired as I
was of it then, I should not have the slightest objection to hear
you sing it again.

I quite envy you the coming dances at Sydenham, and often
think of the last one at Mrs Colchester's. It is most annoying
to hear the bands playing all the old waltzes and know that it
will be long before I can dance to them again.

Sydenham must, by this time, be almost a complete fair with
the people coming to see the new Crystal Palace.[3]

6 : Varna

During June 1854 most of the British expeditionary force left Gallipoli for Varna, the northern Black Sea port in Bulgaria. The divisions embarked in orthodox order: first the Light Division, then the 1st, 2nd, 3rd (less one regiment left behind on detachment), and finally the Cavalry Division. Sir Richard England, commander of the 3rd Division, to which George Lawson was attached, was a pleasant, friendly officer, not strong on initiative and criticised later for slowness in the field, but who did not try his troops unnecessarily: unlike 'that old bear' Sir George Brown, who insisted on everyone wearing the stiff leather stock, even though it strangled them; or General Eyre:

There is drill going on in the Regiments which are in General Eyre's Brigade almost continuously. Sunday is even worse than weekdays, and the men say that it is now, 'six days shalt thou labour and on the seventh have heavy marching parade', that is to say a parade with all their traps on their backs. . . . I am glad to say that I have nothing to do with him.

George sailed on 23rd June after several days of intense activity, loading stores and embarking all the sick that could be moved, for transfer to Scutari – the main base hospital opposite Constantinople – the scene of so much suffering later. It was already becoming a place to avoid.

E   51

At Scutari about 400 sick have already been left in the Hospital, and only 4 Medical Officers to look after them, so you may imagine they have plenty to do. . . . It is expected that one or two of us will be left there in charge of our sick, but I am glad to say that I do not think it will be me, as Dr Forrest [Principal Medical Officer of the 3rd Division] has attached me to himself, and has also given me charge of the medical stores to take to Varna.

The journey to Varna took two days in the *Andes*, 'a fine American vessel' and comfortably appointed.

Once again we shall have the pleasure of eating and drinking in a respectable and Christian-like style. You must, I am afraid, think from what I have often said about our living, that eating and drinking is the chief of our thoughts out here. Such however is not quite the case, but when a person has been subsisting for two or three months on Commissariat rations, which invariably consist of tough mutton and coarse brown bread, the delight with which one anticipates a good dinner is not to be realised by another who feeds well every day.

There was no time to land at Constantinople, which enchanted him, at any rate from a distance, and the Bosphorus even more.

The Bosphorous with the houses and palaces extending along its banks is, without exception, the most magnificent sight I ever saw; we fortunately sailed up by twilight which is the most beautiful time for seeing it. The houses are built close upon the water's edge, so that you might land passengers directly from the boats into the houses; they are all painted in different light colours, and to each house is apparently attached a garden. The whole country, as far as we could see it, was very hilly and covered with trees. All this seen just as the sun was setting, throwing a number of beautiful shades of colour over the whole landscape, formed a sight which is not to be described. . . . We were struck with seeing swarms of a small kind of bird which were flying rapidly just above the surface of the water; these

birds are never seen to rest, but always to be flying in this unsettled state, and the Turks suppose them to be the souls of women whom the Sultan has drowned in the Bosphorous.

At Varna the journey and the dream abruptly ended. George's job was to land the horses belonging to the Medical Department, with the aid of four or five native servants who scarcely understood a word he said. His own pack-animal soon shed its load, and he found himself left with one man

to mend the girth and start all over again, while the rest of
the party rode calmly off to camp.

The British were installed immediately outside Varna, in
a continuous row of tents along both sides of the road leading west out of the town. The camp stretched up to elevated
ground above a lake, about five miles long by one mile
broad, a short distance downstream from a second smaller
lake, both formed by the river Devna, which flowed through
each of them and covered a broad area with water and
marsh. It was not a healthy place. Part of it was said to have
formed the plague cemetery of the Russian Army in 1828–9:
the lower ground consisted of soft, black loam liable to
flood, the higher of light clay from which arose clouds of
fine dust in the summer winds. Despite the advantages of a
plentiful supply of water and proximity to Varna, the
whole area was condemned by the doctors; and frequent
moves took place over the next two months to avoid the
'malarial exhalations and miasmata' rising out of the two
Devna lakes and the morass around them. The Light
Division made four such moves, in an attempt always to
combine access to water with freedom from fever. The third
move to Devna village, several miles further west, was
strongly criticised by Dr John Hall – of whom more shortly
– on the usual grounds: but the observations of Assistant-
Surgeon Cattell of the 5th Dragoon Guards offered the most
likely clues.

There were several excellent springs, and the river water was
also good when we arrived, but the proximity of the troops did
not allow of it continuing so; the horses were watered there, and
kept it constantly muddy; the Infantry washed their clothes and
bathed in it, and to add to the mischief, butchers found it
convenient to throw offal into it, while it still formed the chief
supply for cooking, and what was of far more consequence, was
also largely drunk by men scorched into excessive and constant
thirst from fatiguing duties under an unusually powerful sun.[1]

All the divisions duly struck camp and moved away, the 3rd going to Galata Point, a small plateau overlooking the sea on the south side of Varna Bay.[2] This was a fine, healthy spot, well supplied with water and protected by dense bush. Even so, in July, after three months' good health, sickness smote the entire army like an Old Testament plague – malaria, dysentery, and then cholera. The French, generally well situated in camps north-east of Varna, were no better off. Men died like flies. To attribute the cause to the climate or the condition of the ground was merely an evasion. The worst place of all was Varna itself: with its ramshackle wooden houses, blocked-up sewers and open cesspools, and its slovenly population of 15,000 Greeks, Bulgars and Turks. The place stank. Yet Russell reported sudden and remarkable improvements, thanks to the restless energy of the French, who detailed their men to cart the ordure from off the streets, labelled the houses and the thoroughfares, set up a post office, opened military stores and cafés, and encouraged brisk business of every sort. Within a few weeks sutlers and wine merchants were streaming in from all over the Levant.

The general hospital in Varna, however, was beyond even their powers. This was the usual Turkish barrack, a quadrangular set of buildings with an open central courtyard, so cambered that the drainage did not work, and flanked on one side by privies of immense size. It was occupied jointly by the French and British, and taken over by them in a state of utter dilapidation and filth. Dr Dumbreck, the Scots surgeon sent out from London by Dr Andrew Smith, reported:

No words can describe the state of the rooms when they were handed over for the use of the sick; indeed they continued long after, from the utter inability to procure labour, rather to be fitted for the reception of cattle, than sick men. Myriads of rats disputed the possession of these dreadful dens, fleas were in such number that sappers employed on fatigue refused to work in the almost vain attempt to clean them. . . . Attempts were made to improve the ventilation by removing planks in the roofing, and some of the interior fittings of the wards; the flooring was in part repaired, but the want of available labour, expressly for hospital service, was felt to be a sad impediment . . . and the superintending medical officers could not but repine when they contrasted their own position with that of their allies, for whom an organised corps had executed at once and effectually all the operations necessary to render their portion of the hospital at least habitable.[3]

Dumbreck was painting too rosy a picture of French medical efficiency; but he would have been less than human had he not seized this opportunity of pleading for a 'trained hospital corps'. What came instead, of course, was Colonel Tulloch's Hospital Conveyance Corps of decrepit and drunken stretcher-bearers, who tottered into Varna on 19th July and caught cholera quicker than anyone.

Fortunately for him, George Lawson continued for the time being as medical storekeeper of the 3rd Division, and thus had no duty at the Hospital. He was regularly reminded, however, of the conditions there.

. . . unfortunately Cockburn, who is doubled up with me in the same tent, is attached to the Hospital at Varna where the fleas abound in millions; and when it comes to his turn to sleep in the Hospital as orderly officer, that is to say he is on guard for 24 hours and attends all that is wanted during that time – when he returns, I will not attempt to describe the way in which his clothes, blankets, etc., are covered with them. We are obliged to get the servants to take them off with their hands and kill them before the clothes can be brought into the tent. On one blanket yesterday I superintended the destruction of 33 and then disgusted gave it up as a bad case. I would not have commenced a letter with such an unpleasant topic; but you know that out of the fullness of the heart the mouth speaketh, and as I am now writing by candlelight, with a small dip in the stool which acts

as my table and my bed as my chair, I feel that these troublesome – but at the same time lively – creatures would wish me
to know that they are still here.

Two days after George disembarked at Varna, there
arrived – on 27th June – the new Principal Medical Officer
of the expeditionary force, Dr John Hall. Hall's name is
still execrated in history as a ruthless disciplinarian, a
medical ignoramus, and the principal persecutor of Florence
Nightingale. That he was awarded the KCB in 1856 is
attributed to official whitewash, while many of his deeds
and statements have been interpreted with the same sense
of bias. Hall, like many others in positions of responsibility
in the Crimean campaign, was placed in an almost impossible situation: having to solve problems incapable of quick
solution, deriving from long years of public neglect and the
relatively primitive state of medicine as a whole. He was no
genius as Florence was, and he had no access to the seat of
power at home as she had. He had no social advantages
such as she enjoyed; indeed, he suffered severely from the
inferior position allotted to the civilian departments in the
Army, and the actual contempt with which all 'fighting'
officers – senior and junior alike – regarded men employed
in the supporting services. They were not real soldiers.
With all his faults and disabilities, Hall was essentially a
victim of circumstances; and even his appointment was the
subject of controversy.

It will be remembered that on 10th February 1854 Dr
Andrew Smith had been instructed to see to the medical
requirements of a force of 10,000 men proceeding shortly to
Malta, where it would act as an 'army of observation' and
stand by in case of a declaration of war. Smith acted at
once and, having issued his requisition for stores and
equipment, cast about for a Principal Medical Officer. He
was in luck. Already sitting in Malta was Staff Surgeon

William Henry Burrell, an officer of long service and good record, the very man for the job. Smith gave him the appointment and promoted him to the rank of Deputy Inspector-General. Hardly done, when a new situation arose: the force was going to be trebled in size and sent to Turkey.

This altered the whole position, as Smith knew that for work on that scale a man who held the rank of a full Inspector-General must be put in charge, and that he could not possibly advance Burrell to that rank immediately after his recent promotion, for this would have been completely contrary to the regulations of the Service. He therefore instructed Burrell to proceed to Turkey, there to act temporarily as Principal Medical Officer until the arrival of the man who would be chosen to supersede him, when he would become the second medical officer under him. Though Burrell very much disliked this arrangement, he obeyed orders, and proceeded to the East.[4]

Later Burrell resigned and returned to England with a sense of grievance, to which he gave full play. Meanwhile, Smith had to fill the new post, and chose Hall, then PMO in Bombay. Hall had joined the Army Medical Service in 1815 and spent most of his subsequent career in stations abroad. He did not obtain his MD until 1845; and this has been construed as a reflection upon his professional abilities – but without justification.

It was not unusual at this time for young surgeons to serve in the army or navy for a number of years for the sake of experience and then to take a higher qualification (like the MD degree) if they left the service to enter private practice or, obviously, if they wished to be promoted to a higher appointment within the service. Hall's career conforms to the normal pattern, a pattern which still prevailed during the Crimean War. Of a group of 255 specially appointed medical men who went out to serve with the army, most had as their medical qualification simply a 'surgical diploma' and only 52 the degree of MD. Hall's failure to take an MD until 1845 is therefore hardly a matter of special comment. He had great practical experience, and earned considerable praise for his skill.[5]

Hall sailed from Bombay on 10th May and reached Constantinople on 17th June. His journey is of some interest, as it took place before the Suez Canal was cut. Reaching Suez on 27th May, he travelled by 'van carriage' to Cairo, thereafter proceeding down the Nile to Alexandria. He was a meticulous man, as his diaries[6] show.

At Cairo, if there are many passengers the scramble for accommodation at Shepheard's is very great, and when obtained it is generally dirty and there are no servants to attend you. The table is abundantly found, but the fare coarse and badly cooked, and the charges for wine etc. enormous. Williams' Indian Family Hotel, which is near Shepheard's, is well spoken of by those who have been there.

He stayed at Williams'.

The donkey boys at Cairo and Alexandria are a great nuisance at the Inn doors, and from passengers overpaying them very exorbitant in their demands. About 1/6 is their hire for the day, but they are in the habit of demanding a shilling for the shortest trip. . . . At the Pyramids the fellows try intimidation on the weak-minded and nervous, and generally succeed in obtaining a considerable sum of money from them under threats of leaving them in the chambers into which they have conducted them as guides. Nervous persons should not go alone to these places, nor indeed anywhere else out of the sound of Bow Bells. . . . At Alexandria I saw a strong ruffian, more like a desert robber than a donkey driver, demand a dollar for bringing a gentleman from the landing place to the Victoria Hotel, and although the gentleman gave him 2/– he was so violent and abusive that the Landlord, Mr Ward, was compelled to send for a janissary and have him put in prison.

On 11th June he embarked on the Austrian Lloyd steamer for Constantinople.

Had to put up with a deck passage in consequence of the whole of the accommodation between decks being engaged for the harem of Mahomet Ali. . . . Written directions put on [the luggage] with paste are apt to be defaced or destroyed altogether by the rats and cockroaches.

Passage money from Bombay to Constantinople. Purchase of 3 horses at Alexandria, freight and contingent expenses for them and private expenses – £177 8*s*. Loss by exchange etc. £3. Expenses for outfit for the Field at Constantinople – £100.

The day after his arrival at Varna, he paid his respects to Lord Raglan and the other commanders and then took a look at the Hospital. He was at once confronted with the kind of obstruction that was to bedevil his life for the next two years.

The building . . . is one square of an old barrack, part of which Dr Dumbreck has only been able to get cleaned and made in some way fit for the reception of sick, owing to the small number of sappers out here, and the lukewarmness of some of the authorities on the subject. The place is literally alive with fleas, and quite uninhabitable until whitewashed. Spoke to Lord Raglan on the subject.

On 29th June an officer and party of sappers were sent to the Hospital to clean it up and improve the ventilation, but Hall found the 'establishment in great confusion' and was already apprehensive of the future. On 4th July he noted:

There is a camp rumour that an armistice for 61 days has been concluded, and if so there ends the War, or it is very unwise of the Allied Commanders to put off their operations until the sickly season arrives when half their force would soon be crippled by disease on the banks of the Danube. . . . What would be the use of going to the Danube now except to get fever, and to follow the Russians through the devastated province of Wallachia would be an absurdity. Better far transport the Army by sea to Odessa if they really want to get near the enemy.

As it transpired there was no need to wait for the 'sickly season' in the late summer and autumn, for cholera and the other fevers were in full force by the end of July. On the 12th he visited the Light Division at Devna, where some early cases of cholera had occurred. Fortunately, it was less serious than he feared; the general health of the division was good and the cholera cases soon recovered – but he had mixed feelings about Devna.

Devna is perhaps better supplied with milk etc. than any of the other camps, as the country people have been protected and encouraged and now come with their *arabas*[7] freely and without fear of molestation or any sort of ill-treatment; but even then all the men can obtain are onions, no bad thing to be sure, cucumbers, a few melons; quantities of unripe apricots are brought in daily, which perhaps are rather an evil than a good.

The ration meat is thin and indifferent and the ration bread of an inferior quality badly baked sometimes, and apt to turn sour. There is not a commissariat supply as it ought to be, and salt and pepper are frequently wanting. Sir G. Brown thinks the men can procure salt wherever they go, but the demand would be great and the local supply dear and uncertain in a short time. They ought also in my opinion to be kept and supplied from the commissariat stores.

The position of the camp at Devna is an objectionable one in my opinion and will be seriously influenced a little later from the extensive morass at the head of the lake, which is directly to windward of it. . . . I foresee much sickness in the Army and the Light Division I think is over-drilled. There can be no use in drilling the men daily as if they require that both officers and men should revert to the goose-step.

Soon after Hall got back to Varna, cholera assumed epidemic proportions: at first among the French, but it quickly spread to the British and the Turks, both in the

camps and in the Hospital. Thereafter Hall's diaries become
a regular record of death. British official returns showed that
whereas only 17 men died in June (less than 0·1% of the total
strength), the figure jumped to 379 in July (1·32%, mostly
from cholera) and 852 in August (2·82%). In September,
when the whole force landed in the Crimea, the figure was
858, exclusive of battle casualties (2·83%, less from cholera,
more from bowel diseases). Hall's life became one of nagging
anxiety and ceaseless toil, and all this before any fighting
had taken place.

Several letters from Dr Smith with new inventions to report
on, as if we had nothing else to think about, but the Jims of
quacks and speculators. I am obliged to work 8 or 9 hours a
day at office drudgery owing to the stupidity of my clerk whose
brain is addled. Poor devil, he is willing enough but this is all
new to him; he never ought to have left Chatham where he was
comfortable.

To add to the trouble, staff officers usually forgot to tell
the supporting services of their plans.

Got an order at 9 p.m. to warn a Medical Officer to join a
party of Sappers and Miners at daybreak in the morning who
were going to Rustchuk to throw a bridge over the Danube.
Warned Mr Brown of the 94th. The other people going on this
expedition knew it early in the day, and the Medical Officer
ought to have the same intimation in common fair play.

On 10th August a great fire broke out in Varna. Russell
happened to be absent in Constantinople at the time and
was only able to report at second hand. Hall, however, left
this graphic description:

Last night about half-past 7 o'clock a fire broke out in a
French wine shop near the Port Gate – spread with rapidity –
burned for many hours notwithstanding the efforts of many
thousand soldiers employed to arrest its progress, and consumed
nearly one-sixth of the town. It broke out in the immediate

neighbourhood of the great magazines of grain, stores and gunpowder of the two armies, and is supposed to have been the work of Greek incendiaries. The English grain and biscuit stores were consumed and the French lost a great part of their army stores.

The large powder magazines containing an enormous quantity of powder, which are injudiciously situated in the most crowded part of the town, were preserved with great difficulty. This morning the town presents a scene of desolation not often witnessed; and last night the conduct of the soldiers, both French and English, was very discreditable, and even today the cases of brutal intoxication present themselves in every direction. From the quantity of property scattered about, the appearance of the place is that of a town taken and sacked. It is possible that this diabolic act may have been that of incendiaries, and what favours the supposition is that the fire broke out in two or three places at once; and a man it is said was found with lucifer matches in the neighbourhood of the origin of the fire. . . .

There is a report that lucifer matches were scattered extensively in our own storeyards where forage, stores and gunpowder are accumulated to an enormous amount, and a French officer cut down a Greek attempting to set fire to a house in an opposite quarter of the town. . . .

The sight was magnificent and the risk quite exciting, as there were only a few yards of space between the burning masses and many hundreds of tons of gunpowder. Having gone to see the fire, I laid down and went to sleep, trusting the exertions of the people employed and that Providence would protect me.

On the very day of the fire George Lawson fell ill, and his father was distressed to receive a letter from Dr Forrest informing him of the 'serious indisposition' of his son. He had contracted fever, it was thought, by exposure to the sun after attending a sick officer on board a transport in Varna Bay. The symptoms appeared to abate, but soon delirium set in and poor George wandered about and be-

came incoherent. 'Still', added Dr Forrest disturbingly, 'I
am not without hopes of his recovery.' By the 19th the
worst was over, and on the 23rd George wrote his first
letter home for three weeks; there seemed a strong chance
of his being sent back to England. On the 24th, all danger
over, Dr Forrest wrote again:

I assure you I view his recovery as a most miraculous one,
not only from the violent head symptoms he laboured under,
but from the continued and profuse haemorrhage from the
bowels which prostrated him and brought him to the brink of
the grave.

He had probably had a bout of typhoid fever, induced by
contaminated food.

On 28th August he started writing again in his old style.
He was not coming home after all. Although still weak, he
was gaining strength steadily, thanks to Barclay and
Perkins' 'capital porter' and better rations. Before his
illness, the supply of food had been disturbingly irregular.

The other day I had nothing but some sea biscuits and water
for breakfast, and a few days before I had a similar feed in the
afternoon dinner, and the horses for 2 or 3 days had to go
minus, and very nearly arrived at the same condition as the
horse which the gentleman endeavoured to feed upon air, and
so decidedly fasted.

Later there was a marked improvement.

They give us now rum, an extra ½ lb of meat making 1¼ lb of
fresh meat per day, 1½ lb of bread, rice, sugar, and coffee every
day: while the poor Frenchman has, I am told, ½ lb of meat
only which he makes into soup and under some long name
drinks it, and fancies it is good. The French during their spare
time, however, pick up frogs which are here in abundance,
tortoises, etc., which they cook up to their own tastes, and
sometimes, my Italian servant tells me, they are luxurious
enough to search for snails. I saw a French soldier the other day

with a quantity of frogs in a bag, and he was quietly amusing himself with cutting off the hind legs of the animals while the poor things were still alive. I remonstrated with the fellow for his cruelty, but he quietly smiled – I suppose at my ignorance – and patting his stomach said they were for the cuisine.

The Italian servant was one of a series whom the medicos had to employ and pay for themselves. This was a long-standing grievance.

It is disgraceful that a set of officers should be compelled to do the menial work which we have to do, while all the officers in the Regiments are supplied with soldiers as servants.

George described the Italian as –

. . . shockingly, dirty-looking, unwashed, unshorn . . . who sleeps on the ground and lives night and day in his clothes, passing the night in my tent. As I have each night found him rather a nuisance, being very loquacious, I have ordered a small tent for him, so that in future he may pig for himself. His only recommendation is that he is a good cook, and understands the mystery of the kitchen most thoroughly, and can turn out an omelette as well as at the Hotel Windsor, Rue de Rivoli, or the Trois Frères, Palais Royale.

The Italian had been preceded by a Frenchman, an equally skilful cook, and an old campaigner, having served a French General during the campaign in Algeria. However, even he was not perfect.

He has one great weakness which is the great value he sets on lucifer matches. He has brought with him about 60 boxes of wax ones which are not be spoilt by moisture, and two or three times a day he comes to me to know if I want any of these matches and extols their merits, puts one in his mouth and then strikes it off . . . in fact I am getting rather tired both of seeing and hearing about these wonderful matches.

Convalescing, George found time hung heavily. Camp life was dreary, the heat oppressive, and the temperature swung

wildly through the extremes, due to the frequent thunder-
storms and torrential rain that accompanied them. He had
few illusions about his own appearance. He had had his hair
cropped French style and generally conformed to Lord
Raglan's preference for clean-shaving, although orders were
changeable and conflicting on this point.

Just before I was taken bad, an order came out to say that
all officers were to, or might be allowed to wear a moustache.
Now during the time I was bad all shaving was put aside, the
result was on recovering I found that all the mahogany colour
had disappeared, that I looked rather cadaverous and hungry,
which in fact I always am now, rather white, with a moustache
and a rough Irish-looking grisly beard. The razor has now
brought me to a civilised condition, but the moustache is sacred.

Meanwhile, what of the war? Since the Turks had
checked the Russians on the Danube, 'shaves', or rumours,
abounded. Apart from minor engagements, little contact
with the enemy had been made either by the British or the
French.

It is supposed by many that the English are going to take
Anassa on the Circassian coast. It is said to be a strongly fortified
place with about 30,000 Russians; and that while we are engaged
with this piece of work, the French will take Odessa. The next
shave is that we are going to open up the mouth of the Danube,
and destroy a number of stockades which are about there; and
lastly the one which seems generally to be believed is that, in
some cunning manner, we are going to try our fate at Sebastopol.
. . . Whether this is true or not it is impossible for me to say;
but certainly, I think, we shall not make any advances far up
the country, as one of the Commissariat told me positively that
they could not provide for us this year if we did, that they had
neither the supplies nor means of conveyance, but they could
manage very well for us if we liked to go to Sebastopol.

This shave turned out to be correct, although for a long
time neither the Government nor Lord Raglan really knew

Galata Point, Bay of Varna, where the 3rd Division was encamped

Surgical instruments taken to the Crimea

what to do. The immediate object of the campaign had
vanished – to prevent the Russians reaching Constantinople – thanks to the unaided efforts of the Turks themselves. Nevertheless, two large armies had been sent to the
seat of war, were profoundly bored and disintegrating
through disease. Something had to be done, and to return
tamely home was unthinkable. Ultimately, in agreement
with the French Emperor, the Cabinet instructed Raglan
'to concert measures for the siege of Sebastopol', reputedly
a heavily fortified naval base. Ironically, it had been constructed with British help, but was now regarded as a
standing source of danger to the Turks. Raglan, however,
was allowed the last word – a privilege he hardly welcomed.
No one had the slightest idea how strong the Russians
were in Sebastopol or anywhere else – neither Raglan nor
the other allied commanders, Marshal St Arnaud and Omar
Pasha – and the longer they waited, the harder the decision.
In the end Raglan decided to go ahead. The sea journey
would do the men good, and despite the known inadequacies
of supply and transport, he hoped that all such matters
would be cloaked by the brevity of the campaign. By 19th
July the die was cast.

But it was not until the end of August that any visible
move was made to mount the expedition and assemble the
troops for embarkation. For a short time George was disturbed lest he be forbidden to go. 'It will be very hard to
have to return to England, now that the only chance of
obtaining a medal has occurred.' In the end he overcame all
obstacles and survived a taxing and quite unnecessary false
start.

Two days ago [30th August] we were all ordered to embark at
6 o'clock in the morning, the place of embarkation being 2 miles
distant. We accordingly had to get up soon after 3.0 a.m., as
the tents had to be struck, all the pack horses and arabas laden,
and breakfast to be had. I went down seated on the top of some

F

baggage in a bullock cart, and after remaining on the beach for about 3 or 4 hours, I was told that there was not room for me in the vessel. I consequently had to come back and pitch my tent again. I did not however suffer in the slightest from this fatigue, altho' it was the first time I had been out, that is to say more than a few yards, since my illness.

On 2nd September he succeeded in boarding the *Arabia*, a sailing transport, which was duly towed out to Varna northward to Baltsch Bay, the rendezvous for the fleet. Like everyone else, George was stirred by the magnificent spectacle of the ships[8] – surely an unconquerable armada – and the prospect of action at last. Optimistically he wrote:

I hope that when this affair is over they will send us home – the talk is that we are to winter in Bucharest. We can easily get there by some of the small Danube steam vessels.

The armada sailed at dawn on 7th September – unfortunately, without the ambulance waggons.

7 : The Crimea – a brief campaign?

The voyage was dilatory, but pleasant enough, and as the doctors had hoped it did some of the men some good. On 13th September the western coastline of the Crimea came in sight – it seemed bleak and barren and bereft of life – but the fleet plodded on towards it, and in the afternoon two officers were sent ahead to receive the surrender of the port of Eupatoria. Next day the landing took place, not at Eupatoria, too small to function as a base, but in Calamita Bay, a few miles to the south. The French landed first, expertly and without fuss. They promptly planted a flag on the beach and had a division ashore by midday. The British did less well, yet they got going at last and by the evening large numbers of men had landed. The operation was completely unopposed. Such luck could not last indefinitely; it would have had to be limitless to offset the bad staff work and confusion on board. Besides this, many men were still weak with diarrhoea, and a frightening number collapsed from cholera soon after they had struggled on shore. The dead were well off, for they were buried *in situ*. The sick were carted on to the *Kangaroo* and died later – the first of the overcrowded and under-attended death ships that headed for Scutari, where fresh horrors were in store.

After midday a fine rain began to fall and in the evening a storm broke. The British soldiers, loaded with personal

69

rations, ammunition and equipment, had no shelter. In contrast to their allies, the British authorities had left the tents to last and failed to unload them in time. Moreover, the packs, by order, stayed on board, and did not reach their owners for several weeks. It was a miserable night, and the men huddled together or walked ceaselessly up and down. By comparison, George Lawson did not do badly and described his experiences in his first two letters home. In the second,[1] dated 22nd September, he said he had managed to sleep through it all in the open. In the first, dated 18th September, he mentioned – with unconscious irony and no intended relevance – that the day of disembarkation and discomfort was the second anniversary of the death of the Duke of Wellington.[2] Then:

Our vessel was not relieved of its load until the evening; we landed on a sandy beach and had to march about 2 miles. We brought nothing on shore with us excepting our blankets and great coats; a change of clothes was impossible, as I am not allowed carriage or a baggage animal. We all bivouacked for the night; but as wood could not be found anywhere to make large fires and the night was a pouring wet one, raining in torrents at times, the impression made on my first sleeping out in the open was not favourable. The following night we had tents, but were obliged to sleep in large numbers in the tents; and as we have no beds we sleep on the ground and cover ourselves with our blankets, and with some straw stolen from some of the villages, we really are as comfortable as *can be expected*. We suffer dreadfully from want of water. The first day was very hot; we had nothing to drink but water drained out of puddles from the previous night's rain; and even now the water is so thick that, if put into a glass, you cannot see the bottom of it at all.

Soon a source of water was found, and by good chance a convoy of carts containing corn and flour was captured almost at once. Within a few days, extensive foraging

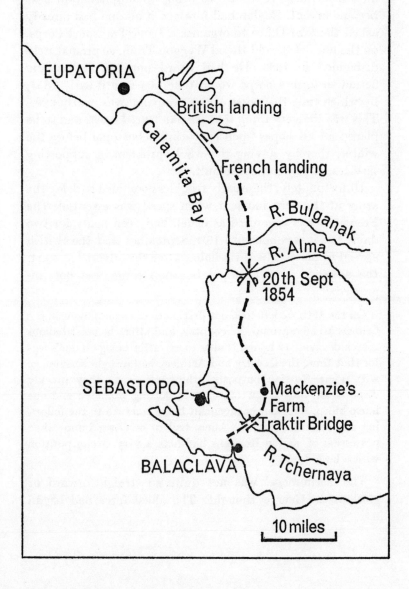

OPERATIONS
14th–24th September 1854

EUPATORIA

Calamita Bay

British landing

French landing

R. Bulganak

R. Alma

20th Sept
1854

SEBASTOPOL

Mackenzie's
Farm

Traktir Bridge

BALACLAVA

R. Tchernaya

10 miles

brought in much more, including a thousand head of sheep and cattle, a number of horses and camels, and over 300 waggons with their teams and drivers. The immediate emergency was allayed, but to live solely on the country was out of the question; and for the first time the need for an army transport service to bring up supplies from base became urgent. Raglan had foreseen it all and had already asked the War Office to organise a Land Transport Corps, on the lines of the old Royal Waggon Train, so prematurely disbanded in 1833. He had heard nothing. Indeed, no action to form a corps would take place until early 1855, by which time the worst of the campaign was nearly over. This was the very thing that Raglan feared most; and so he placed all his hopes upon capturing Sebastopol before the winter, thereby solving the whole problem of supporting services, as it were, by default.

Unfortunately, these early troubles combined to delay the army at the very moment when speed was essential. The French, better organised as usual, had been ready for two days; but it was not until 19th September that the British agreed to move. Then, six hours after the advertised start, the advance on Sebastopol began. George was not impressed:

On the 19th we left this, our first place of encampment in the Crimea, to advance up the country, and after the most tedious march of about 12 hours, that is to say after being on one's legs for that time, the Cavalry and Artillery had a slight scrimmage with some Russian outposts, whom of course they quickly disposed of; only a few of our men getting wounded and one horse killed, a regular engagement being reserved to the following day when a river, the Alma, had to be crossed and taken possession of, as the Russians had here a very strong position with a large force.

The 'scrimmage' was not quite so straightforward or glorious as George thought. The allied force had begun marching at 9.0 a.m., the French and the Turks along the coast on the right, the British inland on the left. The infantry moved in compact masses as on review, flags flying, bands playing, riflemen in the van. The cavalry guarded the open flank on the left and in the rear, and probed ahead not far in advance of Lord Raglan himself, who, followed by his staff, rode well out in front of the main body. The baggage waggons, pack ponies and mules and all the camels, cattle and sheep were led or driven on the inside flank.

It was in this area that George found himself. Medical preparation was slight. When a man was wounded, he walked if he could or – if found – was carried back to the regimental hospital (a bell tent) and there attended to by the regimental surgeon. This officer could not do much, other than apply dressings, staunch bleeding, and carry out minor surgery and treatment. Serious casualties were then conveyed to the divisional field hospital, two or three miles to the rear, out of range of field artillery, where the staff surgeons (such as George) conducted operations. The scheme depended largely upon transport, the very thing that was lacking, since all the ambulance waggons had been mysteriously off-loaded at Varna. The official report admitted afterwards:

It is now pretty generally known that the army landed at the Old Fort [Calamita Bay] with no other hospital transport or ambulance than one pack pony per regiment, for the conveyance of what are called the field panniers – small basket-work cases, intended to contain the surgeon's instruments, a few of the most requisite dressings and appliances, and a few medicines most likely to be needed in an emergency – the whole being limited by the weight-carrying powers of the sorry animal generally furnished for this duty. To this were added ten canvas stretchers per regiment for the conveyance of sick or wounded men on the shoulders of their comrades. For all other means of transport, whether of wounded, of instruments, of medical comforts, or

surgical appliances, the army was left entirely dependent upon
the resources of the country.[3]

'These', the report went on, 'failed to supply what was
needed': which meant that instead of there being available
a convoy of Dr Andrew Smith's ambulance waggons,
manned by members of the Hospital Conveyance Corps,
there was simply a handful of *arabas*, scraped up together
with their owners, or driven by anyone else that could be
found. The fact that two of the ambulance waggons did
arrive after all, together with a detachment of Corps men,
made no difference – as Dr John Hall recorded:

Found two of the ambulance waggons on the beach [at
Calamita Bay] but without either horses, harness or drivers.
Landed the 60 ambulance men from the *John Masterman* with
their bearers [stretchers], but the feeble old men will be of little
use with them. In fact if they manage to take care of themselves
it is as much as they will accomplish. . . . I find that the quib-
bling old Pensioners who were landed from the *John Masterman*,
taking advantage of an order given them by an officer of the
QMG's department to lodge their bearers for the night in the
waggon on the beach, took advantage of it to leave them there
altogether, and I overtook the worthless old fellows, marching
along the road as an armed body. They were sent back . . . but
before their arrival on the beach the waggons, bearers, and all
had been re-shipped. . . .[4]

By the afternoon of the 19th many of the men marching
in the columns felt throttled with thirst; and so when they
came upon the Bulganak river, they broke ranks and
plunged into the water: still, fortunately, without inter-
ference from the Russians who, however, were busy clearing
up the country in the rear and waiting in strength behind
the ridges ahead. The 'scrimmage' reported by George
Lawson was a cavalry reconnaissance, broken off under
artillery covering fire by order of Lord Raglan himself: after

which the Russians retired to a position of massive strength
on the heights beyond the next river, the Alma. It was in
sight of this position that the allies bivouacked for the
night.

The Battle of the Alma has been described so often that
any detailed account would be superfluous here. Suffice it
to say that the battle plan was unimaginative and the
ground tactics little better. The French started the fight by
attacking the lightly defended Russian flank on the coast,
and – after a long check – eventually gained the heights and
their objective. The main battle was conducted on the left
by the British 1st, 2nd and Light Divisions. After fording
the Alma under heavy fire, they frontally assaulted the
Russian redoubts and defences around Kourgane Hill, the
main feature, and by an amazing display of determination
and sustained courage came through to success – though
with serious losses. All the hard work was done by the field
officers, NCOs and private soldiers – initiative and control
at the higher levels of command being at a minimum. Lord
Raglan, however, caused the enemy real consternation by
taking up an advanced position on his own, almost within
the Russian lines. When all was over at 5.15 p.m. the
fighting had lasted nearly four hours. Then came the clearing up. Since the 3rd and 4th Divisions had been held in
reserve, the extent to which George was involved is not
clear. It is likely that, after the battle, he helped fellow
surgeons of the active divisions, where the carnage had been
frightful. He wrote home:

The scene after the engagement, going over the field, and
looking after the killed and wounded, is a sight not to be
described. Many of the poor fellows had to be on the field all
night, not being able to get them off that evening. There was
plenty of work for the doctors.

During the afternoon a common field hospital for the 2nd

and Light Divisions had been established about half a mile
in rear of the centre of the army.

Here the marquees were pitched that had been brought in the
reserve waggons – consisting of six common country carts or
'arabas' (all that could be obtained for this purpose) – such
bedding and comforts as these sufficed to carry were unpacked,
and the medical officers exerted themselves zealously in affording aid. The wounded of the 1st Division were all collected and
got under cover in some houses in a vineyard [in the village of
Bourliouk] near the scene of the action the same evening; but
as night fell soon after the battle ceased, and it became intensely
dark, many men who had fallen on the more distant and broken
parts of the field, were unavoidably left till the following
morning, when strong fatigue parties were sent out to collect
the remainder of the wounded and to bury the dead. A farm
house in the village that had escaped the fire was taken, the
whole yard littered down deep with hay, and here this latter
portion of the wounded, as they were brought in, were placed
– their hurts attended to, nourishment given to them, and they
were then sent down as speedily as possible to the beach, a
distance of three miles, for conveyance to Scutari. The whole
of the British wounded and many Russians were thus disposed
of by the evening of the 22nd.[5]

So ran the official report. Many personal accounts have
added colour to the bare facts so related – the cries of the
wounded pleading for water, the surgeons bloody as
butchers throwing severed limbs on the floor, the dead
dragged by the heels into open pits, the extraordinary behaviour of Russian wounded, who fired on anyone sent to
succour them. The casualties would not have been collected
as expeditiously as they were had it not been for the help
given by parties of British Marines and the French Ambulance Corps. Petty deficiencies, such as candles, caused
fearful havoc, as they prevented surgeons working after
dark. Staff Surgeon T. Alexander of the Light Division told
the Hospital Commissioners later:

On the 20th, when the Light Division had about 1,000 killed and wounded, there were no ambulances, etc., etc., or lights (save the personal property of the officers) – nearly all the operations requiring to be performed on the ground. I, myself, operated the whole of the first day on the poor fellows on the ground, and had performed many on the second (two of them being hip joint cases), until an old door was discovered, of which we made a table, and of course performed all my other operations (including another hip joint case on a Russian) on the same.[6]

Alexander also praised the French and the Navy: had it not been for them, 'Heaven only knows how we could have had our wounded moved to the shipping'. Yet this constituted the very next stage in the story of horror. There were plenty of ships, but none had been adapted for the purpose of carrying casualties;[7] in short, there were no proper hospital ships, and no trained staff or stock of medical stores kept ready for such an emergency. Inevitably chaos followed, and first-hand accounts of overcrowding, filth, stench and utter misery are too numerous to mention. A sober, less horrifying and thus a more intelligible report was rendered by a naval surgeon, James Peters, of HMS *Vulcan*:

On the day of the battle, this vessel, with many others, was at anchor a short distance from the field of battle, but no notice was given to me that sick or wounded would be sent here; consequently no preparation was made for their reception. But early next morning a small steamer came alongside with 86 soldiers, in charge of an assistant-surgeon of HMS *Agamemnon*; six of these had been wounded in the cavalry skirmish the night before the battle, and had suffered amputation. No document nor order about them was sent, and I considered that no others were coming, and proceeded to arrange them on the main deck. . . . I was for some time without any assistant, but about noon boat after boat came alongside with the sick and the wounded, and I was obliged to ask for a signal to be made for

surgical assistance. . . . About 6 p.m., finding that there were
nearly 500 on board, and that others were alongside, I requested
the first lieutenant, in the absence of the commander, to prevent
any others coming on board. . . . Of course with so large a
number of men pushed on board so quickly, any arrangement
was out of the question, and with the exception of those first
brought on board, the sick and wounded were placed indis-
criminately on the decks, to the great risk of the wounded, for
with diseases such as cholera and dysentery extensively prevailing, the atmosphere becomes quickly tainted. But the
marines and seamen of the vessel, albeit rough nurses, behaved
in the kindest manner to the poor creatures. But great distress
was experienced from the want of urinals and bed pans, one
only of each being on board; and from the want of these, many
blankets were thrown overboard by my order when they became
foul.

In conclusion, I would say that, although I do not feel called
on to blame any one . . . there can be no doubt that, as from the
time the army landed in the Crimea a battle was impending and
sickness was very rife, some arrangements should have been
made, and certain vessels fitted for the purpose.[8]

It was not surprising that Dr John Hall, as Principal
Medical Officer in the Crimea, and Dr Andrew Smith, as
Head of the Army Medical Department in London, were
singled out as convenient scapegoats. Who else could have
been responsible for what was purely a medical matter? The
truth, of course, was less simple, and so less convincing.
As explained, the causes of the chaos were numerous,
various and elusive: stemming from public neglect of the
Army, departmental red tape, and the ridiculous gulf –
social as well as professional – fixed between the fighting
arm and the supporting services. There was little hope of
solution at this stage of the campaign, and as yet Russell's
dispatches to *The Times* had not fanned public indignation
to a white heat; but it was this that was to hasten the
arrival of Florence Nightingale and lead ultimately, after

protracted commissions and enquiries, to necessary changes.

Meanwhile, the rigours of a Crimean winter would have
to be endured to the full, a prospect unaccepted and concealed, for Raglan had every intention of advancing at
once and capturing Sebastopol before the bad weather set
in. Unwilling to pursue the enemy at the tail end of the
battle, he planned nevertheless to thrust on immediately
afterwards with a force composed of cavalry, horse artillery
and the 3rd Infantry Division; but was prevented from
doing so by the surprising obstinacy of the French. Marshal
St Arnaud, a dying man and an indifferent soldier given to
dramatic gestures and sonorous statements, refused to co-
operate, and he repeated his refusal for the next two vital
days. The reasons are immaterial. Raglan's fault lay not in
his unreadiness, but in his constitutional inability to get
his own way. Over-sensitive towards others – a fatal defect
in a commander – he was weighed down with the feeling
that he must preserve the alliance at all costs: indeed, he
had received express orders from the Government to do so.
It was, however, a disastrous sentiment, and instead of
having it out with St Arnaud he concealed his chagrin and
impatience, for he was convinced that he could not take
Sebastopol alone. The enemy seemed still too strong, and
reinforcements were already said to be arriving from south
Russia. And so he waited, while the battlefield was cleared
and the wounded taken to the ships.

On 23rd September the allied armies moved off at last,
morale high. Sebastopol would soon be theirs: a wish transformed into conviction when later in the day they gazed
upon the town, glittering on the far side of the estuary, the
roadstead filled with ships. On that side lay the principal
buildings, including the dockyard and other naval installations, and in their capture and dismantling lay the whole
meaning of the war. On the near (north) side there was only
one area of military interest – a group of barracks and store-

houses dominated by a star-shaped fort (the Star Fort),
gunned and equipped for all-round defence. Which way to
go? Raglan wanted to take the Star Fort first, contending
that its capture would very likely lead to the surrender of
the town. Even if it did not, it would be an asset of great
value, enabling the allies to sit astride the main road to the
north and cut communications with Russia proper – one
reason why the town held out so long, for in the event the
Russians were never surrounded nor fully besieged, but
managed to keep this lifeline open. Once again St Arnaud,
now almost dead from cholera, opposed Raglan; but so did
General Burgoyne, a Royal Engineer of age and renown,
who produced a string of reasoned arguments as to why it
was better to march round Sebastopol and attack it from the
south, where the defences were incomplete, the direction of
assault unexpected, and a handy base available in the
harbour of Balaclava nearby.

It was a nice balance of time *versus* place, and place won
– a disastrous decision. There was only one way to win the
war before the winter – to attack at once at the nearest
point before the Russians were ready. The march-round
incurred delay, and involved the allies in a whole new set
of tactical and logistic problems which took months to overcome; meanwhile, the Russians lost no time in consolidating
their defences. Raglan had been right yet again, but – too
nice – he allowed himself to be overruled. That was fatal.

8 : Sebastopol saved

On 24th September the flank march round Sebastopol began, the British leading. The operation took two days and was skilfully done. Way had to be forced through dense woods and thickets in hilly country, and direction kept by compass. Raglan felt they were all in acute danger, as the two armies were cut off from the coast and the fleets at sea, and were open to attack from north and south. In fact, there was small risk. The Russians were dispirited and in full retreat. Their rearguard bumped the British on the Sebastopol-Simpheropol road at a place called Mackenzie's Farm; otherwise there was little contact until the British captured Balaclava, almost without a shot, on the 25th.

Unaware of all the doubts and decisions of the commanders and the opportunity missed to seize Sebastopol by a *coup de main*, George Lawson merely recorded his displeasure at having to do so much marching. On 3rd October he wrote to his mother from the 'Heights above Sebastopol', viz. outside Balaclava:

The unfortunate 3rd Division has been marching and countermarching every day. . . . Why this unfortunate Division has been so much more run about than the others I cannot say, but I suppose it is that not being very actively engaged at the battle of Alma, they are to be the attacking party with the 4th in this present siege. One day we had a very heavy march, and were

81

left on a hill about 5 miles from the rest of the army, to act as a
rearguard until the French came up to take our place. This they
did about 12 o'clock at night, and we had then to commence
another march to get up with the army. We arrived at 4.0 a.m.,
not starting until nearly 2, and at $\frac{1}{2}$ past 5 we had to be off
again for another day's work; this has been the hardest bit of
work in the way of marching we have had yet. Another night
we were encamped in a wood. The whole march has been up and
down, over a very high hill and thro' valleys. The Russians
burn all the villages and compel the inhabitants to quit them,
and when we arrive we seldom find more than a smoking mass
of ruins. Had they not been about the most cowardly race of
beings on the face of the earth, we never could have arrived at
where we are now with the most splendid positions. They have
never offered the slightest resistance to our march . . . if they
had but retired from one hill to another and kept up a small fire
on us, I am sure they would have so reduced our army as to be
unfit for the present attack. In one of our marches we were
accidentally led beneath some batteries, which opened fire on
us in a fierce manner with shell and round shot. This is the
first time I have been thoroughly under fire, and altho' I hear
daily now from Sebastopol plenty of the whizz of shot, I do
not yet at all admire the sound.

Balaclava was a small fishing port, crouching under steep
cliffs, on the east shore of a narrow inlet of the sea. The
water was deep enough for big ships to come right in and
tie up; but the small size of the harbour and the lack of
lateral space – the maximum width was 250 yards – was a
severe restriction. Use by both allied armies was out of the
question. Having got there first, the British decided to stay,
and so compelled the French to take over the two shallower
harbours of Kamiesch and Kazatsch further up the coast
towards Sebastopol. In the event the French profited
exceedingly, as it meant once again that both their flanks
were covered: the left by the sea, the right by the British.
The latter, on the other hand, were saddled, as before,

SIEGE OF SEBASTOPOL.—DR. SMITH'S NEW HOSPITAL WAGGONS

Embarking the sick at Balaclava

with one flank in the air: a dangerous situation which
proved a constant anxiety and a drain on manpower,
since Raglan had to find sufficient troops both to conduct
the siege and to guard against a Russian attack from
inland.

For the time being, however, prospects were bright and
hopes still high. Although the nights were beginning to turn
cold and there was a scarcity of tents, during the day the
weather remained good. At first too there was plenty to eat.
The farms and orchards were fruitful and untouched, firewood was available, and the inhabitants seemed friendly:
though it did not take long to strip the countryside and so
hasten an unwelcome return to the ration issue of salt beef
and biscuit. But what kept every man on his toes was the
immediate thought of winning the war. With few exceptions, soldiers and commanders alike were convinced that
Sebastopol would fall within forty-eight hours; and there
was a very good chance that it would have done, provided
an attack had been launched with speed and determination,
losses notwithstanding. Defences on the south side of the
town were as yet negligible, and the garrison was small and
ill-armed. The main Russian army under Prince Mentschikoff lay defeated and discomfited outside, and was
unlikely to have intervened with effect.

Raglan was quite ready to go in, but once again he was
opposed by the French. St Arnaud, on the point of death
(he died on 29th September), had been replaced by General
Canrobert: a capable commander, but unwilling to venture
his troops in another pitched battle so soon after Alma.
Any assault needed protection by covering fire, and in his
view the field artillery was insufficient. Siege guns and heavy
ordnance must be awaited, and again General Burgoyne –
an expert in caution – took the French side. For the third
time and for the same reasons Raglan gave way. In his
view, only a combined attack could achieve success and the

G

alliance must be preserved at all costs. So the third chance slipped away: there was no fourth.

Three whole weeks then followed, from 25th September till 17th October. During that time the allies hauled up their guns and dug trenches, while the Russians transformed a 'thing like a low park wall'[1] into a powerful defence system, running all round the southern side of the town and re-inforced by six solid redoubts. The driving force behind the defence was Vice-Admiral Korniloff, and the brains the engineer officer Lt-Col Franz Todleben. Men, women and children worked night and day beside the soldiers and sailors, digging ditches, building walls and ramparts, siting guns. On 9th October 28,000 troops moved in to strengthen the garrison; and still the allies did not attack.

George Lawson, like most others, was still hopeful and confident, but impatient at the delay.

Since my last letter home little in the way of taking Sebastopol has been done, that is to say the siege has not yet been com-menced, but both sailors and soldiers are all busily engaged in landing the siege train which will be, when the guns are placed in position, the largest that has yet been ever brought against any town. We now surround the whole of one side of the town. On the hills and the entrenchments which are to be thrown up there will be placed 190 of the largest guns in Europe, which will all open fire at one time; some of them, it is said, to be placed within 600 yards of the town. Many of the guns will be firing red hot shot while others are pouring in shells.

When this is all to take place it is difficult to say. We have now been here 8 or 9 days placed under fire of the Russians, and apparently doing nothing, wasting all the splendid weather with which we have been favoured. I hope this will not continue much longer, as all are not only getting tired of being in the Crimea, and existing in one suit of clothes and sleeping on the ground, but also are beginning to dislike being made for so long targets for the enemy, allowing them quietly to build up batteries and try the ranges of their guns on us. When once we do commence,

I have no doubt but that we shall soon quiet them. . . . Tents
are now being issued to the men, so that it appears as if we are
likely to remain here for some time yet.

The French are for the most part comfortably situated in the
rear, and are throwing up earth batteries and mounting their
guns, as it is expected that there is a very large army of Russians
coming up to strengthen Sebastopol. We shall all however have
the advantage of them this time, and have the hill which they
will have difficulty in passing; and the unfortunate Russians will
probably meet the same fate as they did at Alma.

Brave words, but the anxiety underlining them is obvious.
Five days later, on 12th October, he wrote in the same vein:

We are still encamped in the same place as when I last wrote:
Russians more annoying and troublesome with their round shot
and shells than ever, and instead now of only firing during the
day as they did for the first week, for the last three nights and
days they have kept up an incessant game, hardly ceasing during
the whole time for above half an hour. As they had a difficulty
and, in fact, they found it impossible to level their guns
sufficiently to reach us, they threw one of their vessels in the
harbour on one side, and from this – and it is supposed one of the
Tiger's guns[2] they are able to throw their shells a great distance.
The reason of our being now so much more disturbed than we
were, is that now working parties are out every night making
the entrenchments, and all the necessary preparations for the
guns which are being rapidly placed in position, ready for us to
commence the attack on Sunday morning.

Russians are continually escaping from Sebastopol and giving
themselves up as prisoners to the English. This afternoon a
Russian sailor has just made his escape from one of the vessels in
the harbour and given himself up – on account, he says, of
having received a flogging on board ship last night for not having
turned out quick enough. His back being rather mutilated, he
has been sent to one of our hospitals. He says that the Russians
intend holding out as long as possible, but that they do not think
that they have a chance of saving the place, and as soon as they

find the game is up with them, vessels in readiness will take them
across the harbour, and they will be off escaping by the side of
the town which is not surrounded with English and French
troops.

While morale was still intact and life relatively pleasant
– at least where the 3rd Division was encamped – George
gave the impression that all was fairly well behind the lines
as well as forward:

We are in good health compared with what we were in Varna,
and during the whole time we have been on the hills above
Sebastopol, only one or two cases of cholera have occurred. . . .
The place where the vessels disembark all the provisions is at
Balaclava, where the sea runs inland for about half a mile
between high rocks on each side, and so deep is it that in parts
there are no soundings. The *Agamemnon*, one of our largest
men-of-war, lies close up to the road side and you are able to
walk, by means of a plank, from the road to the vessel. A
small village is here, which when we first came was entirely
deserted, but latterly Greeks and such like disreputable people
filled the houses and opened shops, which proved a great comfort
and advantage to all. But the other day, it is said, a letter was
found recommending some of the Greeks to set fire to the place,
as they had done at Varna. Lord Raglan consequently had
them all turned out, and now the village is as empty and
deserted as it was when first we came to it.

What George did not realise was that Balaclava was fast
becoming a hell-hole. As the sole advance base of the
British troops engaged in the Crimea, it received all reinforcements, ordnance and supplies and discharged all
casualties. The harbour did not hold sufficient ships; the
shore installations were inadequate and there was not
enough flat ground for all the new ones that were needed.
Besides this, the road up to the plateau where the troops
were stationed was so narrow and poorly surfaced that –
during the winter – it was to turn into a terrible track of

death. The traffic was heavy enough already; and Captain
L. G. Heath, RN, of HMS *Niger*, temporarily assigned to
shore duty, recorded a vivid impression:

The road is covered with conveyances of all sorts – Crimean
bullock or camel waggons, Turkish bullock waggons brought
from Varna, Maltese mule carts from Malta, all with provisions,
etc., and artillery waggons with shot, shell, or fascines and
gabions; then comes an occasional aide-de-camp at a gallop, or
an infantry officer, dusty and weary-looking, returning from
Balaclava laden with whatever he has been able to buy – some
preserved meats or a bottle of brandy, perhaps three or four
ducks, or a pound of candles. He looks quite triumphant as he
passes you with his prize. You can have no idea of a campaigning soldier if you have only seen them in St James's Park or in
a garrison ball-room. They live in their full dress coats, and the
consequence is the scarlet has turned to port wine colour, and
the gold lace and epaulettes to a dark coppery colour; the coat
is generally full of holes, and the individual wears no shirt.
The change of life to them must be very great, and some of them
feel it a good deal.[3]

Nor was George aware that, although the 3rd Division
had a fair bill of health, other formations had not; and it was
their sick that were already flowing into and flooding the
two small buildings assigned for their use in the town. The
diary of Dr John Hall, who arrived at Balaclava on 26th
September (the day after its capture), tells the story.[4]

Sept 26: Here there is a harbour for shipping and accommodation for 150 sick. . . . The hospital is fitted with bedsteads, there
is bedding and other conveniences. . . . A [school] building was
found in the town that had been used as an hospital and in it
was found a pharmacy containing a number of useful medicines.
244 sick sent in to the hospital at once, many of them moribund
from cholera. 10 men died in the course of the night.
Sept 27: Sick continue to pour in from the division labouring
under cholera and fever. 350 in hospital, application made for
a ship to put them in.

Sept 28: 420 sick and more still pouring in from all quarters.
Sept 29: Accommodation on shore quite full.
Sept 30: Sickness continues to prevail in the whole army from
exposure at night, and cholera is particularly destructive among
the newly arrived troops. I have urged the necessity of the men
having tents, and I believe they are to be found immediately.
At present all attention is absorbed by the landing of material
for the siege of Sebastopol which will commence in two or three
days now and is not expected to last more than a week. Have
got some stores landed from the *John Masterman* transport
and am to have hospital marquees pitched at once.
Oct 1: Admitted since our arrival here 490, died 50 – no abate-
ment of sickness. Sent off sick since the army landed in the
Crimea 700 sick and 1,500 wounded.[4]

On this day Dr Hall was ordered at one hour's notice to
embark for Scutari, to investigate alarming reports concerning conditions in the General Hospital there; and he did
not return to the Crimea until after the bombardment of
Sebastopol had begun on 17th October. Scutari is not the
business of this book. George Lawson never served there;
while the epic of the General and Barrack Hospitals is
indissolubly associated with the name of Florence Nightingale, who arrived early in November. Scutari is, of course,
relevant in that it was the base to which all severely sick
and wounded were sent from the front: and this impinged
on the character of the hospital at Balaclava. In that
context, and in the conditions of transit across the Black
Sea, it will play its part in this narrative.

Meanwhile, everyone – from the Commander-in-Chief
downwards – took refuge in the thought that the situation
could not possibly last. The bombardment would settle
everything. And George, making the best of it as usual,
concluded his last letter home to his father before the great
event with:

Thank Mother for her letter which I have received by the last mail. All letters are, I assure you, most gratefully and thankfully received. They arrive and are delivered to us with tolerable punctuality. I have no cause to complain, as I think I have received 12 letters since I have been in the Crimea; some, however, had been very long on the road, some of them bearing dates early in August. I am unable now to pay my letters, as Queen's Heads are not to be bought at present, or rather I cannot get to the Post Office to buy them, and money is not taken by the Letter Serjeant.

I must now conclude with love to yourself, my Mother, Aunt, Uncle, Mary, the girls and all at home including the Old One[5] and Believe me ever to remain

Yr Aff son

Geo Lawson

9 : Bombardment and battles

At last at 6.30 on the morning of 17th October the bombardment began. Although the Russians had been well aware of what was coming, they did not know the date and time; nor for that matter did the allies, who only made up their minds the day before. The fire plan was simple. For maximum shock and tactical surprise, all the land batteries were ordered to open up simultaneously and continue in cannonade from nearly 120 guns. Unfortunately, the initial effect was diminished by the fact that the Russians fired first: even so the allied artillery made a mighty impact, and although thick smoke soon obscured the targets and made it difficult to assess results – or even to aim with accuracy – it became plain as the day wore on and Russian return-fire weakened that great damage was being done. George wrote to his cousin Mary:

The game commenced this morning, and at $\frac{1}{2}$ past 6 a.m. 100 of our heavy siege train guns opened fire upon the Russian batteries. Nothing can be seen at present, even when close, except a mass of smoke, but I believe, altho' they have been now at it only about six hours, they have done considerable damage; certain it is that the Russians do not now return the fire in the same fierce manner as they did at the commencement. The large round tower which has been so long troubling us with shells, is now disabled. In a few hours the ships will come in

close and open their broadsides into them. They were unable to
come in sufficiently close before, on account of some batteries
but which are now permanently destroyed. I have been up on
the stone quarry, which is near our entrenchments, and where
the generals are stationed, but from the smoke etc., you could
not make out much that was going on. Fortunately for us they
do not seem to be doing much damage amongst our men, as we
have had very few wounded. Soon after they commenced this
morning one of the French powder magazines blew up, which
considerably impeded their work for some time.

The naval part of the bombardment proved a great disappointment. Owing to various vexatious delays, the ships
did not begin firing until the afternoon and then – despite
a great show and sound and a vast expenditure of ammunition – they made but small impression on the solid stone
forts that protected Sebastopol from the sea. Very few
defenders were killed. On the other hand, all drawn up in
line, the ships were sitting targets for the Russian guns,
which took toll both of vessels and of men.

Elsewhere, however, the Russian situation was deteriorating. The defences facing the British on the SE side of
the town were disintegrating under the relentless fire, and
an assault was expected at any time. None came. The
reason was simple – the British were ready, the French
were not. At a greater distance from the Russian batteries
and suffering fewer casualties, the British were in good heart
and keen to attack. By contrast, stationed close to the
Russian lines on the left, the French had taken the brunt
of the enemy fire and sustained heavy loss. The men were
discouraged and needed a respite to rebuild their emplace-
ments. As always, Raglan refused to attack alone; and so
at dusk the bombardment came to a dead stop – unfulfilled.
During the night, with great energy, the Russians repaired
the battered defences and brought up fresh guns, so that on
the following day the whole thunderous process had to be

gone through all over again. And that was the pattern for
the next week – bombardment all day, not followed by any
attack; repairs and raids at night. It was an endless overture
that benefited the Russians far more than the allies. The
former improved their position by digging reserve trenches
and strengthening cover, thereby reducing casualties. The
latter consumed their resources and, by exposure, suffered
the more; above all they seemed no nearer to capturing
Sebastopol. Moreover, their own defensive position was
intrinsically weak, especially the British; and it was only a
question of time before the Russians took advantage of it,
for their main force under Prince Mentschikoff still lay
outside the town.

On 28th October George wrote to his mother:

On the morning of the 25th, three days since, the Russians
came down in large numbers upon Balaclava, and succeeded in
getting at one time close upon the town or village. The 93rd
Highlanders received them in a most gallant manner, they had
formed in line and were charged at by the Cossacks. As soon as
they had arrived within about 100 yards they gave them a
volley of Minié[1] bullets, and then prepared to receive them on
the point of the bayonet. Whether the Cossacks did not like the
appearance of these bare-legged people I do not know, but they
immediately turned round and bolted. The Turks, miserable
wretches, behaved badly. They had charge of two batteries with
14 guns, and when the Russians came up to them they ran to a
man, leaving our guns in their possession.

Such was George's impression of the first part of the
Battle of Balaclava, and it was reasonably accurate. The
port was mainly defended by six redoubts, equipped with
naval guns and manned by a force of Turks. These redoubts
were sited beside the Woronzoff Road that ran along the
so-called Causeway Heights above Balaclava itself. Apart
from the 93rd Highlanders and a detachment of Marine
artillery in final reserve, this was the sole force defending

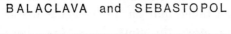

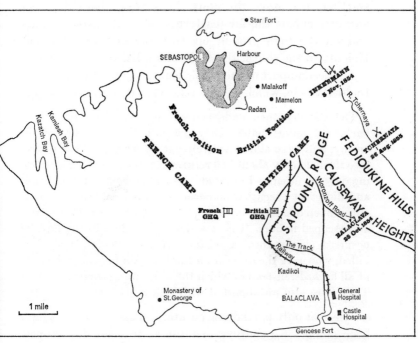

the British Army base. Sir Colin Campbell was in command. Just before dawn on 25th October, the Russians attacked in strength the most easterly of the redoubts, and after an hour's sturdy resistance captured it. Soon afterwards, finding themselves unsupported by their allies, the Turks abandoned the other five redoubts and headed for Balaclava. Russian cavalry then charged the 93rd Highlanders almost at the entrance to the port, but were repelled as George described. By this time reinforcements were beginning to arrive, and the Cavalry Heavy Brigade under General Scarlett drove back the main force of Russian

cavalry, which had advanced along the North Valley on the
further side of the Causeway Heights. Meanwhile, the
Russians had taken four out of the six redoubts and were
starting to remove the guns. They were also siting men
and artillery at the far (eastern) end of the North Valley
and on the high ground on both flanks – the Causeway
Heights to the south, the Fedioukine Hills to the north.

The second part of the battle concerned the Charge of the
Light Brigade, which George related in the following terms:

The Cavalry then endeavoured to take them [the guns]
back, but unfortunately they got into the cross fire of the
enemy, and were almost entirely cut up. Out of 600 who went
into the field only about 150 returned. Some regiments numbering only 30, others – I am told – less. They behaved most nobly
and did great execution amongst the Russians, but they were
outnumbered and got surrounded. Lord Cardigan led the charge
and escaped unhurt. It is said that the mishap to the Cavalry
occurred chiefly thro' a mistake of an Aide-de-Camp, since
killed, who gave the order from Lord Raglan to charge the guns
at all hazards, instead of which the order was a conditional one.
They were also unsupported with either Artillery or Infantry.

This was only partially accurate. Indeed, arguments have
been going for a century or more as to what did happen,
although the main sequence of events has now become clear.
When the Heavy Brigade was fighting its way through a
Russian force five times its size, the Light Brigade under
Lord Cardigan waited inactive on the flank; and was much
criticised for doing so. The fault probably lay equally with
Cardigan and Lord Lucan, the Divisional Commander. The
two men were brothers-in-law, socially superior, proud and
stupid; and they hated each other. Their enmity cost many
lives. Able to see over the whole battlefield – which the
Cavalry generals could not – Lord Raglan then sent Lucan
an order to recover the redoubts, promising infantry support
from divisions now coming up. Not seeing the infantry any-

where, Lucan still hesitated; and so, deeply impatient, for the situation was slipping and the Russians were actually towing off some of the captured guns, Raglan sent him a second order 'to advance rapidly to the front – follow the enemy and try to prevent the enemy carrying away the guns . . .'. Captain Nolan, ADC to General Airey, the Chief of Staff, brought the scribbled order at full gallop, but was maddened by Lucan's inability to understand it. He, Lucan, could not see the redoubts and, partly due to natural inertia, had no idea of what was going on. All he *could* see was the far end of the North Valley, where the Russians had massed their guns and a large force of cavalry. When Nolan flung out his arm in that general direction, more as a gesture of annoyance than anything else, Lucan's worst fears were confirmed. Thus – instead of attacking the Russians in the redoubts to the south – he ordered the Light Brigade to charge the whole length of the valley towards the wrong guns. As a result men and horses were cross-fired both ways by enemy artillery sited on the flanks, in addition to frontal fire from the guns ahead, and lost about two-thirds of their strength. The charge became a legend, but it was certainly no victory, nor was the Battle of Balaclava as a whole; yet there had been some fine feats of fighting and – despite heavy losses and mistakes – morale remained high. It made not the slightest difference, how-ever, to the situation before Sebastopol, which George rue-fully admitted on 2nd November had not yet fallen. Later in the same letter he gave a most disturbing hint:

I am sorry to say that there is great talk of our wintering here; whether it will turn out to be true or not, I do not know, but I sincerely hope not. The weather here is at times very warm, at others very cold. We have had 3 intensely cold days with strong north-easterly winds in which we were all very miserable, cross, and wish to be home again; we then have fine weather again for a short time, and then our 3 days' misery. Warm clothing, it is said, is to be sent out for the soldiers. I hope they will not forget the officers. The poor fellows now are sadly over-worked, not having one whole night out of 4 for their rest, as they are either on guard or in trenches. It is now frosty in the night and morng, but very fine during the rest of the day. If we do not have wet, I have no doubt that we shall do very well.

There were, however, a few consolations:

As for myself I never was better, getting very fat, and feeling very jolly. I should not however object to being sent home with sick and wounded when this affair is over. I think I am now senior in length of service in Turkey of all the Staff Asst-Surgeons who came out here, and therefore may stand a good chance. I must not calculate on such good luck. Dr Forrest, myself and another officer sleep together in one tent. I have now my baggage, and indulge myself by placing my mattress on the ground, so that I am at night very comfortable. In fact during the cold weather bed is the most comfortable place, and as soon as it becomes dark we turn in, and have our grog in bed, and read the papers *when we have any* by candle light. We are never hardly later than 8 o'clock.

Today, in passing thro' the French camp, I saw the band practising. The little men, even out here, cannot do without their music, and you can hear the band playing in the distance every night. Our band is used out here to carry the wounded from the field, and attend to the sick etc.

The Russians, however, had not given up their plan to bring the allied armies to battle, and so force them to raise the siege of Sebastopol. On 26th October, the day after the Battle of Balaclava, a Russian force of 5,000 men issued from the east side of the town and made a strong recon-naissance towards the British right. They entered a broken, hilly, terrain of ravines and plateaux, thick with under-growth, and reached Shell Hill, a historic height that was to figure in the fighting to come. There they were driven off by the British 2nd Division, holding the extreme right of the allied line – the engagement being known as 'Little Inkerman' after the ruined village on the opposite side of the Tchernaya valley, and as the forerunner of the main battle on 5th November.

During the next nine days it was obvious that the Russians were assembling in strength in this area, and a close watch was kept. Rain fell heavily on 4th November and into the night, when no hostile movements were reported; and it was not until the pickets were actually coming off duty at dawn on the 5th that the first Russian attack came in. This was the beginning of a combined attack by two large forces: one of 19,000 men under General Soimonoff from Sebastopol, another of 16,000 under General Pauloff from beyond the Tchernaya. Both converged towards the area of Shell Hill, approaching along the ravines on either side. A third force under General Gortschakoff was directed down the Tchernaya valley to engage the French division stationed in the hills above the Plain of Balaclava; while a fourth tactic consisted of a demonstration by the Sebastopol defenders to pin down the main French forces on the left near the coast.

The British defence was composed – from right to left – of the 2nd Division, the Guards Brigade, and the Light Division: aided during the day by the 4th Division, detachments of the 3rd, and certain French units. Although heavily outnumbered and sometimes short of ammunition, they succeeded in driving back wave after wave of Russian attacks, and just managed to hold on to a handful of key heights and strong points. Like Alma, it was another soldiers' battle. Raglan took a few important decisions, but left almost all the tactical action to the formation commanders, and they in turn relied heavily on the field officers, NCOs and men to fight it out as best they could in a heavy blanket of fog. Once again it was a matter of individual initiative and aggressive courage on the part of a

smaller force, repelling a great weight of material and a
mass of men, who had not been trained to fight independently
and who were too numerous for the constricted nature of
the ground. By mid-afternoon it was all over, with the
Russians in full retreat. There was no pursuit. The British
lost 2,500 killed and wounded; the French 1,700; the
Russians over 12,000. It was the last battle before the
winter – which was to take a far heavier toll of life than
any hostile engagement.

George wrote home on 7th November:

The 5th November here was kept up in great style and, I am
sorry to say, turned out much such another as at Alma. The
Russians in immense force . . . attacked us on the right; the
outposts were engaged as early as 4.0 a.m. and at 6 o'clock the
work commenced in earnest. The fighting lasted until nearly 3 or
4 o'clock, and terminated in our giving the Russians a great
beating. The loss on both sides was, as you may imagine from
the long time they were engaged, very great, but Russ. suffered
much more than we did. It is believed that they numbered
50,000 and were repulsed and well routed by the French and
English numbering only 12,000. They had 32 and 24 pounders
while our Field Battery had only 9 pounders. Our loss . . . is
almost as bad as at Alma. In this case the wounded were all
removed from the field, had their wounds dressed, and on a
soft good bed and had had either some warm tea, or beef tea,
as the case required before 9 o'clock in the evening.

To judge by Russell's dispatch, the reality was less rosy
than George realised. Russell went over the battlefield two
days after Inkerman, when stretcher-bearers were still pick-
ing up wounded and burial parties were hard at work, and
told *The Times*:

Litter-bearers, French and English, dotted the hillside, now
toiling painfully up with a heavy burden for the grave, or with
some subject for the doctor's care; now hunting through the
bushes for the dead or dying. Our men have acquired a shocking

facility in their diagnosis. A body is before you; there is a shout, 'Come here, boys, I see a Russian!' (or 'a Frenchman', or 'one of our fellows'). One of the party comes forward, raises the eyelid if it be closed, peers into the eye, shrugs his shoulders, says quietly, 'He's dead, he'll wait', and moves back to the litter; others pull the feet, and arrive at equally correct conclusions by that process.[2]

George continued:

You may imagine that all the doctors had enough to do. Our Division [the 3rd] had only two regiments engaged and consequently did not suffer nearly so much as some of the others. I had consequently to lend a hand in the 4th Division, which had suffered most severely of all, losing their General [Cathcart] and one Brigadier, the other wounded, besides a great number of officers killed and wounded. They buried 14 officers yesterday. In this engagement I was well in the rear receiving the wounded, and as I am a non-combatant, it is in my opinion the best place in the field. Our men behaved admirably, many of them smoking a little black clay pipe during the engagement, came back 3 or 4 times for fresh supplies of ammunition; and when they had filled their pouches carried away some in their pockets for their comrades who were running short of it.

I am not able to write much tonight as it is near bed time, and I am tired having been engaged during the day taking into Balaclava the sick and wounded to put on board ship for Scutari.

10 : The winter begins

The excitement and euphoria generated by the Battle of Inkerman soon evaporated. Within a few days reaction was biting deeply into the Army, as one unpalatable fact after another had to be faced. First of all, while everyone had been ready to endure anything so long as Sebastopol was taken quickly, this had not happened; and the High Command was squarely blamed for the inexplicable delay before the bombardment and the failure to assault while it was going on. Secondly, not only had Sebastopol become strong, but the Russians had already passed to the offensive and fought two pitched battles (Balaclava and Inkerman) in addition to numerous minor engagements and aggressive sorties. There was no knowing when they would attack in force again. It had become only too clear that the siege would now last well into the winter, and that this would have to be spent in the open on the heights above the town. Moreover, the weather was bad enough already. How much worse would it get? Lastly, even if supplies of the right kinds arrived quickly and in abundance, there was little chance of their reaching the troops for some time – to judge by the chaotic condition of Balaclava and the appalling state of the track up from the port.

The outlook was bleak indeed, and when related to the decline of the British Army in strength and health, it

100

seemed near to desperation. Already on 24th October – the
day before the Battle of Balaclava and nine days before
Inkerman – Russell had reported:

The diminution of our numbers every day is enough to cause
anxiety. Out of 36,500 men borne on the strength of the army
there are not now more than 16,500 rank and file fit for service.
Since the 10th of this month upwards of 700 men have been sent
as invalids to Balaclava. There is a steady drain of some forty
or fifty men a-day going out from us, which is not dried up by
the numbers of returned invalids. Even the twenty or thirty
a-day wounded and disabled, when multiplied by the number of days we have been here, becomes a serious item in the
aggregate.

George, as usual, did his best to sound cheerful:

It is now one week since the battle of Inkerman was fought.
. . . The wounded are now all sent away from the camp and put
on board ship for Scutari . . . in other respects there is not much
alteration, Sebastopol still remaining untaken, indeed in artillery it is far stronger at present than we are, and where we fire
one gun they will discharge ten, their supply of guns and
ammunition being very great. Many of our guns are disabled,
I believe about 30. . . . It is said that Lord Raglan has sent to
Constantinople and Malta for more siege guns and as much
ammunition as can be had. Fresh arrival of troops, both English
and French, are also daily expected. The general opinion now is
that we are to winter here, warm clothing is on its road for the
men, and charcoal is already being landed in Balaclava. We
shall thus you see in time have an enormous army out here, and
if the weather is not too severe so as to disable the men, I do
not think there can be much doubt as to the fate of Sebastopol.
I am sorry that there is so little chance of our getting in
there for winter quarters, as we should then be comfortably
housed.

He did not disguise the severity of conditions in the front
line:

The poor fellows who suffer most are those men who are down in the trenches when it rains. They go down for 24 hours and take their food with them. They are obliged to keep close in as the shot and shell are continually passing over their heads, and when they are relieved and return to their tents, thoroughly drenched and tired, they have no change to put on, as clothes (altho' reported to have arrived) have not yet been issued out to the men. The result of course is a great increase of sickness whenever the 3 or 4 days' rain comes on. I have been fortunate enough not to have been sent down to the trenches yet. The Assistant Surgeon of the Regiment has always to go in his turn, which comes sometimes once, sometimes twice in a week, and as I do not fancy lying in a deep ditch for 24 hours, with the chance of getting knocked over, I do not volunteer.

In camp it was little better:

You cannot imagine anything more uncomfortable than wet and cold weather in camp. The ground here when it rains is in some places almost as bad as a marsh, and the wet tent does not form a cheerful place to go into, particularly as there are no chairs, or any fire, in fact nothing more than the canvas walls and a few large boxes of medicine which we make use of for seats. Another little inconvenience likewise arises on these days, the difficulty of cooking your food, as all cooking is done in the open air, and the wind either almost scatters the fire or the rain puts it out; but bad as the weather has been we have managed to do pretty well and so must not grumble.

His hints about clothing and food and many other things became more and more pressing and direct:

Will you please give my Mother a hint that a hamper of eatables would be very acceptable here, and if she should send one ask her to put in a good plum pudding which would only require boiling, or otherwise if best, some mince meat, hams, cheese such as Gloucester or Cheshire, and the rest I will leave in her hands. Also put in a pair of fleecy wool stockings for

the night, such as I used to have. I shall shortly write to you
to ask you to execute a quantity of commissions for me as I
am short of trowsers etc.; in fact I am almost now without
them. . . .

Within a fortnight he was writing again:

In case any of my letters may have gone down or miscarried,
I will tell you that in one of them I asked my Mother to be good
enough to send me a parcel of tongues, hams, cheeses, a good
plum pudding, some mince meat in a large jar, and some warm
socks, directed to me, *3rd Division of the British Army, Crimea*,
care of Charles Grace Esq., Pera, Constantinople, to be forwarded. . . .

Another request – itself a revealing comment on the lack
of security on both sides – was:

Will you also be kind enough to send me a map of the Crimea
with the forts etc. well marked out in Sebastopol, I see them
advertised at Wylds in the Strand. You can choose which you
think best and send it by post.

As autumn deepened into winter, the need for clothing
filled letter after letter:

The men are now very badly and insufficiently clothed owing
to their not having received any warm clothing since they have
been in the Crimea. In this respect we are all badly off, officers
as well as men. I have only the one portmanteau which I had at
Varna, as I was not allowed then to bring more on being
obliged to leave my two others at Scutari. . . . I am consequently,
like everyone else, badly off for raiment and thick boots. If you
would send in one parcel half-a-dozen flannel shirts, 12 socks,
and six pairs of drawers I should feel obliged. Also would you
please send me out *two* pairs of waterproof India rubber trowsers
to be bought at Cordings in the Strand, No. 231 I think, as
Dr Forrest wants a pair himself and I told him I would get
them for him . . . be sure and let them be big enough. On 8th of

next month I shall get a Treasury Bill for £50 and send it home
. . . as we cannot possibly spend money here. . . .

There were, however, a few compensations:

We are now encamped close to the Commissariat and I can
assure you that we, that is Dr Forrest and his staff, fare far
better than any in camp. Instead of drawing our exact 1 lb of
meat and other rations of tea etc., the butcher, who is an old
patient of mine, allows us to have (of course quietly) whatever
we like to ask for. The result is that instead of having salt beef
and pork, when all the regiments are on salt rations, we have
our tough beef and mutton as at other times when stores are
more plentiful. Latterly during the last two weeks, owing to the
bad weather and state of the roads, the Commissariat have been
unable to get up their full supplies, and the tea and sugar have
not been issued; but we have supplied the deficiency by buying
these in Balaclava.

The French also always seemed to be better provided and
consequently in better heart.

The French are very pleasant neighbours; they are encamped
behind us and on our left, and they always have their band
playing two or three times a day. Even when a sortie from the
Russians is taking place in the trenches, you will hear the French
playing away as unconcerned as if nothing was occurring. They
are now well provided with warm clothing; coats which they call
'moutons', they are capital things, they are nothing more than
sheep skins, dressed with the wool on, and they certainly are the
proper clothing for out here, as they are very warm and strong.
I wish our men had something of the sort. . . . Many of them
are almost shoeless and shirtless, their great coats worn to a
thread and torn in all directions, having had not only to live in
them during the day but sleep in them by night, covered only by
the wet blanket which they have just brought up with them from
the trenches. . . . I succeeded the other day in buying a pilot
coat from a sailor, and this I luxuriate in, envied I can assure
you by many.

Adversities do not come singly. Inefficiency alone did not account for the deterioration of conditions on the Heights, for on 14th November a catastrophe had occurred.

When we went to bed, the evening before, we were all congratulating ourselves on the nice quiet fine night, and hoping for a continuance of such weather, but unfortunately our hopes were not to be realised, as about 6 o'clock the following morning we were all awoken by a tremendous slapping of the tent in which we were sleeping, caused by the wind having suddenly risen, and in a short time were all obliged to leave it, as it was evident it was falling – and on getting up such a scene presented itself. Every tent was blown down, all the hospital marquees level with the ground and the unfortunate sick lying exposed to wind and wet. To attempt to put them up again was impossible, as the wind was so high that no one was able to keep his legs, even the horses could not hold themselves up, and all the arabas and means of transport we had were turned over on their sides. Camp kettles, soldiers' clothes and saddles were all to be seen flying before the wind; and to complete the misery of those poor fellows who were sick, and exposed from the hospital marquees coming down, it rained and hailed hard at intervals, the weather all the day being excessively cold, the thermometer not standing higher than 40.

We were more fortunate than our neighbours, as by hanging on to the curtains of the tent, and continually pegging the ropes down we succeeded in a way of keeping ourselves under cover. So violent was the wind that those tents which had not their poles broken, were ripped up rendering them quite useless for further service. At about 1 o'clock things began to assume a more moderate aspect, and then it commenced snowing, the wind however still remaining very high, but by dark it had sufficiently abated to allow of those tents which had not been too much injured to be again pitched, and we were then able to procure our first meal, as during the whole day we had been obliged to subsist on biscuit and cheese, and some rum and water which we fortunately had by us.

After a day of this kind one would have thought that the

Russians out of pity would have let us be quiet in the night, but such was not the case, as they attempted a sortie from Sebastopol, and our unfortunate men had to be roused from their tents; of course they were immediately driven back and the men retired to their sleeping places again. Several of the men, from exposure, have since died – or rather had their death hurried as some were in hospital at the time. The artillery lost several horses. But unfortunately our loss did not end there, as I am told that sixteen vessels were wrecked, and on the morning following the hurricane nine were seen aground total wrecks, some distance on the other side of the town of Sebastopol. 12 of the vessels, it is said, are English, the rest French. 4 of them were full of Commissariat stores and one, the *Prince,* full of warm clothing, medicine and medical comforts for the troops. On board this vessel was Dr Spence,[1] a Deputy Inspector-General of Hospitals; and only 3 of the crew were saved. Dr Spence had, I believe, come out from England on a commission to ascertain the truth of the libels told against the Medical Department, and unfortunately went down in this vessel. We are consequently now without supplies for a time in tea and sugar; but as there is plenty of meat and biscuit, and luxuries such as vegetables to be had in Balaclava, we shall not starve yet. The weather has now cleared up and, as after a storm there is always a calm, today we have a fine summer day, and everything now has the same appearance as before.

The hurricane came so suddenly on Tuesday that many very ridiculous scenes presented themselves. In many cases an officer was first made aware of the condition of the weather by finding his tent blown away from him, and himself left in a condition approaching nature on the ground, and had to run and catch his clothes which were running fast away from him before the wind. . . .

The weather has taken up so much paper that I have but little room to tell you much about Sebastopol. *It is not yet taken* but we are still trying to take it, battering away at each other with long guns. . . . The Generals talk very confidently of taking it and hope to be in before Christmas Day. I hope we may and that I may eat my dinner on that day under a roof, and have for part of it some of the good things I wrote for in my last letter. I have not received many letters lately, I suppose in consequence of the rough weather – but always write when you can, as a letter is the only thing *next to grub* worth receiving out here. . . .

11 : Cold, disease and death

LETTERS: 27th NOVEMBER 1854 – 18th JANUARY 1855

The hurricane did not only blow down tents. It blasted the last vestiges of hope for a quick end to the war and almost extinguished the Army's morale. From that time on men no longer joked about the cold or the rags they wore or the eternal beef and biscuit they had to swallow. George had been right about the *Prince*. It had been driven on the rocks at the entrance to Balaclava harbour, and gone down with the very things the troops needed most – greatcoats, boots, underclothing, and a quantity of drugs and purveyors' stores for the Medical Department. At this juncture a shipload lost of guns and ammunition would have been a trifle by comparison. Although, after the hurricane, the sun did reappear now and again, and there were even mild spells, the weather had definitely broken and the winter set in. Rain, hail, snow and high winds were the common accompaniments to the daily round of trench duty and camp life, interspersed with iron frosts and drenching thaws. Indeed, it was the very variability of the climate over the next three months – mid-November to mid-February – as well as the extremes of temperature that made it so hard to bear.

In his quarterly report, Dr John Hall recorded:

November . . . on the 14th, a hurricane, such as is seldom witnessed, set in, with heavy rain, early in the morning, continued

108

all day, and terminated in snow and sleet in the evening; on the 15th, distant hills were covered with snow, and cold was severe; on the 16th, 17th and 18th the weather was moderate; on the 20th there was constant and heavy rain; the 21st was cloudy; from the 23rd to 31st, there were incessant storms of wind and rain from the south-east and south-west, which rendered the grounds and roads ankle-deep with tenacious mud and almost impassable.

December: for the first 6 or 7 days there was rain daily, with snow on the distant hills; from the 7th to the 14th was fair; on the 21st, 22nd and 23rd heavy rain, with distant mountains covered with snow, and a very cold wind blowing from the north-east; 24th rain and sleet; 25th severe frost; from 25th to end of month, weather fair.[1]

The record was continued by Dr Brush of the Scots Greys:

January was ushered in by storms of wind and snow, and the cold was also most intense during this month; towards the end of the first week the thermometer in my bell tent, which was lined, stood at 8 a.m. as low as 18F, and in the single tents it fell as low as 15; this in the cavalry camp situated near Bala-clava, where the temperature ranged much higher than on the heights before Sebastopol where, I believe, the thermometer on one occasion fell to 12F. I never experienced anything so trying as the north-easterly winds which prevailed during the month – the cold blast seemed to search the very marrow – no woollen clothing could keep it out, unless rendered waterproof. Mackin-toshes and sheepskins were alone proof against it, especially the former, worn over warm clothing.

During the month of February the weather was very change-able and trying; during the first week or ten days the cold was severe, accompanied with occasional falls of snow, then we had a few summer days, and the last half of the month was charac-terised by excessive variability in the temperature, the thermo-meter ranging in the bell tents from several degrees below freezing point to between 60 and 70F.

The weather during the month of March was remarkably fine and mild. . . .[2]

Against this background of climatic discord, George made the most of his life, physically and mentally. As he freely admitted, he was better off than some, although no one stationed on the Heights and living in a tent had a comfortable existence. His family were anxious to hear every detail.

You asked me if I still slept on the ground? On the march I did for nearly the whole time under Dr Forrest's tent, but after we had been in our present encampment for about a fortnight we were able to get up our baggage and I secured my bed and portmanteau; but so accustomed was I to the ground that it was 5 nights before I put the mattress on the ground to lie on, feeling that I should not sleep comfortably. . . .

Now with regard to my duties, these are numerous as are the duties of all Staff Assistant-Surgeons; they are a sort of stop-gap, and do miscellaneous work and that which does not belong to a Regimental Surgeon. If any Regimental Assistant dies or goes away from any cause, a Staff Assistant does duty with that Regiment pro tem. I have however been very fortunate. I have always been with Dr Forrest and have charge of medical stores and issue them out to the regiments. I have to attend to the sick of the Commissariat and Staff, with their servants, of this Division; also to attend when ill the arabagues [*araba* drivers], mule drivers, etc.; and when an action takes place, I have either to go into the Field with my panniers – and of course keep in the rear if you can to look after any Staff wounded – or else, as I did at Inkerman, stay at the Field Hospital in the rear, and assist and take your share of the operations, amputations, etc., of which there are far too many. . . .

On 2nd December he wrote:

During the last fortnight, or now nearly three weeks, we have had a succession of wet days and nights, the roads consequently in a most terrible state, indeed the camp is little better. You can hardly walk from one tent to another without getting your feet thoroughly wet, the whole place being almost a swamp. . . . I for one have not had a dry shoe, or rather boot, to my feet for the whole of this period, and as pipe clay amongst the soldiers is entirely done away with, and all the men are in the same suit of clothes as when they first landed in the Crimea, and those they had worn at Gallipoli and Varna, you may easily imagine the picturesque objects they are now. . . .

I need hardly add, after telling you all this, that we have a great deal of sickness in Camp. The regiments which suffer most are those which have just arrived, and not having been seasoned in the way the old troops have, they fall ill immediately from the exposure to which they are subjected from the first night they land. Amongst the regiments cholera has broken out very severely, and many of the old soldiers have also suffered from it. On the 29th November we lost 47 men in one Division and 87 in the whole Army. . . .

Fortunately, the cholera abated as the year ran out, and everyone was cheered by the news that warm clothing and other comforts were on their way from England, although as it turned out nothing ever seemed to get further than Balaclava.

I will now tell you how we managed to pass Christmas in camp. Christmas Eve was a miserable day, hard rain and cold winds, and towards the afternoon some sleet and snow. The roads of course were in a very bad state, so bad as to render it impossible to bring up the full allowance of rations for the men on the following day. We celebrated the evening of that day in our tent with the usual glass of grog, not perhaps quite as good as you were then drinking at Forest Hill. On the following morning, on getting up, we found the ground covered with a thin layer of snow, and that there had been a hard frost during the night. Our little mess had taken good care to secure a good dinner for the day, and we had a plum pudding made as good as our material would allow, and a piece of roast beef, washed down with port wine and ration rum.

Christmas was not the only reason for a cheerful letter, as George now had the faint chance of a move.

You will be surprised to hear that Dr Forrest has left us. He received orders to proceed to Scutari to take the Medical Superintendance of that station. The Scutari Hospital has been much grumbled at, and from the number of sick now rapidly being sent down there, it requires a man of good capabilities to take charge of the place. Had he been there before, there would never have been a complaint against the place. . . . He has kindly promised to have me removed there, but this I am obliged to keep to myself, as it requires some management to get sent down. I shall first get sent down to Scutari with wounded and sick, and he will then detain me there and give me, as I have asked him, one of the surgical wards. When once there you may consider that I am gradually working my way home, as I think it is not unlikely but that in the spring he will send me home in charge of invalids.

George's hopes, however, were not so easily fulfilled. Meanwhile, the New Year ushered in what proved to be the worst month of all. January 1855 was the coldest of the entire campaign, yielded the most sick and the least rations, and remained in men's minds as the very pit of the Army's misfortunes.

Yesterday was an exceedingly cold day, the ground in the morng covered with snow; and the country – now barren and entirely deprived of all brushwood and trees with which it was covered when we first came here – presents a most desolate wintry appearance. The wood has all been cut down by the men for firewood, they have now to dig up roots to get sufficient fuel to cook their rations. Some better arrangement ought to be made. The men, wet and tired out, come up from the trenches in the morng, and many of them have then to seek for wood to cook their breakfasts. Charcoal is now allowed and each man is entitled to so much per day, but the difficulty of bringing up even the biscuit and salt meat, renders it impossible to bring up charcoal in quantities sufficient for the use of the men. Many of the officers benefit from it, as they have their own horses to send down to Balaclava for it.

I am myself well, I am afraid getting rather too stout, but in perfect health, neither cold nor damp seems to affect me, and in this weather in camp we have both. My hair is in a deplorable condition, but a small quantity remains, the result of fever of course. I am not yet bald, but the hair is very short and scanty. . . . A hard steel pen and very cold fingers will account for parts of this letter being rather illegible.

Presents are not to be found here. Balaclava is only able to produce at a very high rate a few articles of clothing and second-rate articles for feeding; you will therefore allow the enclosed [Treasury Bill] to be placed in the family fund. . . . I have also enclosed a small amount to be divided between the girls and Mary to help keep them in gloves during the jovial part of the year. Dances, I suppose, are as usual going on, but we hear little of such proceedings out here. You will, I am sure, have a dance at Forest Hill this year.

Each successive letter told a similar tale.

For two days after writing my last letter to you, there was continued rain and sleet, varied now and then with a little hail. Last night this changed to snow and this morng, on getting or rather waking up, we found inside the door of the tent and extending two or three feet inwards a quantity of snow. On looking out we discovered the ground well covered. . . . Imagine the condition of the poor fellows in the trenches, their clothing first getting wet thro' and then freezing on them, they have now to sit up to their knees in snow. . . . Russ, with this state of affairs, has taken to fire more than ever.

This morning in the middle of a heavy snow storm . . . the French brought their mules to convey about a hundred of our sick to Balaclava. I really pitied the poor fellows, many of them too ill to walk, lifted into the easy chairs slung on each side of the animal's back, and others placed in couches hung in the same manner, to be carried nearly seven miles on a bitter cold morng, snow the greater part of the way beating in their faces.

I have not yet heard any more of my being sent down to Scutari, I am afraid on account of many Medical Officers being sick; and consequently our number of efficients being few in the Crimea, they will not let one who is now well seasoned to the climate to get away.

So severe is the frost that, from your breath during the night, we find icicles all over our blankets in the morning, and many men who have long beards awake with them frozen. My boots and trowsers are always, or rather have been for the last 4 or 5 morngs, in a perfectly rigid state. Imagine the comfort of this in camp, picture yourself encamped on Blackheath when the snow is 2 feet deep on the ground, to have no food but what you can bring from London, and totally unprovided with horses or means of transport, and then imagine that every 2nd or 3rd night you have to sit for 12 hours in a trench filled with snow.

A Dispenser of Medicines has been sent up to our Division. Part of the work which I have had to do, and by far the most disagreeable, viz. the charge of Medical Stores[3] will be taken out of my hands. I shall therefore, in a few days probably, be attached to a regiment, indeed Dr Pine,[4] our Principal Medical Officer, has told me so. . . . I shall now have to do trench work.

George, however, was in luck, although Scutari was as far off as ever. Instead of having to sit every other night in a trench as he had feared, he was to receive orders on 17th January to report to Dr Anderson, Principal Medical Officer at Balaclava, and there to take charge of sick officers sent down for treatment to the General Hospital. He was never to serve on the Heights again.

Vivid as his letters were of life in the Crimea, George was never able to tell the whole story of suffering: indeed, the situation was both better and worse then he knew. The worst of it was that, in January, out of a total strength that rarely exceeded 30,000 men, only about one-third was fit for duty. And of this third many who were ill by ordinary

TURKS CONVEYING THE SICK TO BALACLAVA.

Huts and warm clothing for the army

standards could not, or would not, report sick when the hospitals were full and the lines had to be manned. The best of it was that 'the worst' lasted a relatively short time, and that improvements – once they began to take effect – converted a desperate situation into at least a tolerable one.

Official records for the whole war (March 1854–March 1856) produced some unexpected figures. Deaths from all causes totalled just under 21,000, of which 2,755 were killed in action and 1,761 died from wounds, or 4,516 in all, not a high proportion and not a great number for two years' warfare. On the other hand, disease (not associated with wounds) accounted for 16,297, or nearly 80% of the dead. Of this total, 4,512 died from cholera, 5,950 from diseases of the bowels (diarrhoea and dysentery), 3,446 from fever (typhus, typhoid and malaria), 644 from diseases of the lungs (pneumonia, bronchitis and tuberculosis), and 1,745 from other diseases (including scurvy and frostbite).[5]

The course of mortality was analysed, also the cause and other contributory factors.

Between March and June 1854, when stationed in Gallipoli and recently arrived in Bulgaria, the Army was reasonably healthy, losing less than 1% of strength. However, most of the main diseases had already made an appearance, and by the end of June cholera had assumed the proportions of an epidemic, killing nearly 1,500 men in the following three months. Mortality abated immediately after landing in the Crimea, but intensified in November and December when, as George noted, fresh troops suffered the worst. The disease then declined steeply until a second epidemic occurred in the hot weather, when nearly 1,400 men died between May and August 1855; after which cholera gradually disappeared. The doctors decided that the main cause was a combination of heat, 'tainted air'

I

deriving from stagnant water and night dews, and general filth: hence their insistence on siting camps in high and dry situations – enjoyable in summer, but in winter subject to extreme cold and exposure, and this in turn attracted other troubles.

Virtually all the other diseases worsened with the onset of the winter of 1854–5 and declined in the following spring and early summer. Diarrhoea and dysentery held the record with over 2,000 deaths in January 1855 alone and over 1,200 in February: officially attributed to the effects of exposure, exertion, and insufficient and unsuitable food and clothing in extreme temperatures. Fever killed more than 2,000 in the four months January to April 1855, when diseases of the lungs were also at their worst, although on a lower scale. Other afflictions accounted for more than 1,000. The causes were described in similar terms in each case, but scurvy (a traditional campaign disease) was put down to the lack of fresh vegetables, and to the fact that a ship-load of lime-juice 'brought by the *Esk* in the early part of December, by some oversight was not rendered available to the troops until the early part of February 1855, although medical officers were urgent, if not clamorous, in their applications for this article[6]'.

The following Table of Deaths[7] applies to the critical months:

Month	Cholera	Bowels	Fever	Lungs	Other	Total
October 1854 .	273	157	69	16	116	631
November . .	423	351	63	20	93	950
December . .	651	882	138	41	144	1,856
January 1855 .	71	2,033	512	117	352	3,085
February . .	12	1,230	687	113	439	2,481
March . . .	Nil	512	579	70	216	1,377
April . . .	5	136	307	35	51	534
TOTALS . . .	1,435	5,301	2,355	412	1,411	10,914

The total of deaths (10,914) for the whole period repre-
sented about 35% of the Army's total strength. Apart from
the second epidemic of cholera which followed in the summer
of 1855, the four months December 1854 to March 1855
were the worst, with January the peak period of all. The
official report made no bones about it:

In the month of January 1855 the health of the army rapidly
deteriorated. During the preceding month its sanitary condition
had been daily becoming more and more unsatisfactory, under
the conjoint influence of a pestilential constitution of the
atmosphere, and the excessive hardships and difficulties of a
siege carried on in the winter season; but henceforward, although
cholera had nearly ceased its ravages . . . the climate became
extremely severe, the conditions of the service . . . were marked
by still increasing sufferings, privations and exposure, and under
every class of disease, with the exception of cholera alone, the
mortality more or less augmented. The total deaths amounted
to 3,076,[8] while the proportion of deaths to strength was 9·49
percent . . . thus illustrating the terrible, appalling, and almost,
if not altogether, unparalleled result, of an army *being nearly
decimated in a single month.* . . .

The report went on to say that, paradoxically, the main
cause was not really disease at all, but the 'unhappy
artificial conditions directly and essentially at variance with
the preservation and persistence of human life'. In other
words, conditions caused disease – which is hardly illuminating and looks like some sort of absolution for the medical
profession. But it added correctly that

. . . the mortality which occurred in January and the two
subsequent months was not the result simply of conditions of life
as applied during these months, but was in a great degree the
effect of previous hardships, exposure, etc. . . .

In the final analysis, however, whose fault was it? Sheer
physical misery and despair had to find an outlet against

some official person or body of authority; and there were
two obvious targets. The Commissariat, which supplied the
rations, comforts, clothing and other non-war-like stores,
and organised the transport; and the Medical Department,
which looked after the sick and wounded. There was also
of course the Commander-in-Chief, Lord Raglan, himself.

12 : Whose fault was it – the Commissariat's?

Before the hurricane in mid-November, when conditions were already bad but still bearable, even Russell was inclined to stand up for the Commissariat.

Mr Commissary-General Filder deserves the greatest praise for his exertions in supplying our men with food. The stories which have been circulated respecting the insufficiency and irregularity of the supply of meat, biscuit and spirits, are base calumnies. No army was ever fed with more punctuality, and no army, I believe, was ever so well fed under such very exceptional circumstances as those in which we are placed. We are fed by Balaclava alone; thence comes our daily bread. It has to be carried out day by day, and yet no man in this army has ever been without his pound of good biscuit, his pound and a half or pound of good beef or mutton, his quota of coffee, tea, rice and sugar, or his gill of excellent rum, for any one day, except it has been through his own neglect. We draw our hay, our corn, our beef, our mutton, our biscuits, spirits, and necessaries of all kinds from beyond the sea. Eupatoria[1] supplies us with cattle and sheep to a moderate extent; but the commissariat of the army depends, as a general rule, on sea carriage. Nevertheless, large as are our advantages in the excellence and regularity of the supply of food, the officers and men have had to undergo great privations.[2]

Even before the failure of the bombardment, and while everyone still hoped that the capture of Sebastopol would solve all the problems of winter, the authorities at home had received stern warnings of what might happen. Lord Raglan had asked long before for the recruitment of a Land Transport Corps, and latterly pleaded for bulk deliveries of hay and fuel. On 7th November he took matters into his

own hands and sent an officer to Turkey to buy timber for
hutting. On 13th November Mr Filder himself apprised Sir
Charles Trevelyan at the Treasury of the inadequacy of
Balaclava as a port and base, and said in plain words that
the track up to the camp would become impassable after
heavy rains. Next day came the hurricane, and emergency
measures were at once taken to try to salve all usable
wreckage and to purchase afresh large quantities of stores
that had been lost. SOS after SOS was sent home. Meanwhile, gangs of soldiers and hired labourers were drafted to
mend the track – all in vain – for the weather and the
weakness of the men nullified their efforts. In Balaclava
itself all was confusion, and the port became a chaotic as
well as a stinking hole. The quays were choked with
ordnance and other stores, dumped anyhow, anywhere.
Mountains of goods lay about in the open, damaged and
disintegrating under the relentless rain. The sea itself was
afloat with bales and boxes, offal and corpses. For a time
no one seemed to take command or care, and even after a
measure of order had been introduced Balaclava continued
to appear a turmoil of woe, muddle and mud.

Russell commented on 1st December:

As to the town itself, words cannot describe its filth, its
horrors, its burials, its dead and dying Turks, its crowded lanes,
its noisome sheds, its beastly purlieus, or its decay.

It was at this moment that the majority of men gave way
to despair and vented angry accusations against their
fellows. The Commissariat was nailed for hopeless inefficiency and wastage: but specifically for
    the lack of food, and the dreary unappetising diet;
    the shortage of clothing;
    the senseless stores system, tied so tightly with red tape
        that nothing could be issued (even if available) with-
        out a multiplicity of forms and signatures;

the transport muddle; and, of course,
favouritism and corruption.

George Lawson's letters have already testified to the
state of rations and clothing; and as late as 22nd January
1855 Russell added this characteristic note:

We are astounded, on reading our papers, to find that our
authorities in London believed, on the 22nd December, that
the coffee issued to the men is or was roasted before it was
given out. Who has hoaxed them so cruelly? Around every tent
there is even yet a fair sprinkling of green berries trampled
into the mud, which the men could not roast. There is, however,
some attempt made *out here* to roast coffee at last. Mr Murdoch,
chief engineer of the *Sanspareil* has mounted some iron oil
casks, and adapted them very ingeniously for roasting coffee;
and they have just come into play at Balaclava.

This device was entirely due to the initiative of Captain
L. G. Heath, RN, who had been given command of the
Sanspareil and nominated Captain of the Port late in
November. He recorded in his memoirs:

Somewhere in the end of November or beginning of December
I directed an experimental roasting machine to be made by the
Sanspareil engineers out of empty oil barrels, and this was
worked by *Sanspareil* men, burning wood as their fuel, and it
roasted in one day sufficient for one-third of the army. I then
made two more machines, and turned the three over to the army
to work for themselves.[3]

It was Heath who gave the lie to Russell when the latter
reported, soon after the November storm:

Will it be credited that, with all our naval officers in Balaclava
with nothing else to do – with our *embarras de[s] richesses* of
captains, commanders, and lieutenants – there is no more care
taken for the vessels in Balaclava than if they were colliers in a
gale off Newcastle? Ships come in and anchor where they like,
do what they like, go out when they like, and are permitted to

perform whatever vagaries they like, in accordance with the old
rule of 'higgledy piggledy, rough and tumble', combined with
'happy-go-lucky'.[4]

In January 1855 Heath sent a circular to all the masters
of transports and other steamers, and asked them frankly
what they thought of the system he had introduced for
regulating the movement and berthing of ships. He had
forty-seven replies, all testifying to the efficiency of his
methods. Later he left a memorandum for his successor as
harbour-master, in which he described in detail the arrangements for piloting vessels in and out, and the order of the
wharves. This is interesting, as it gives a clear picture of
how the harbour worked:

The berths opposite the first open space on the Eastern side
. . . are kept as much as possible for the cattle ships; the smaller
ones can land their cargoes (with the assistance of light brows)
directly on to the wharf, the larger ones can do so with the
assistance of the double boat or floating wharf. This saves much
time as the cattle walk on shore.

The next landing place is Ordnance Wharf, where shot and
some descriptions of ordnance stores are usually landed. From
thence up to the head of the harbour are a number of small
projecting landing places, variously appropriated by the Commissariat to the different articles of provisions. Bread, rum,
meat, etc., have each a place appointed to them. The last wharf
at the end of the town is solely for embarking sick. Opposite to
it is a canvas building for their reception, if they should be
detained whilst waiting for boats.

On the Western side of the harbour is a small plot of ground
enclosed by rocks, which is the Navy dockyard, and useful for
hauling up boats, storing driftwood, etc. The Engineers have a
sawpit there, and are working up the large driftwood into
sleepers for gun platforms.

The tugs and small steamers can go alongside the next –
called the Vesuvius Wharf. All troops are disembarked there.

Sheers are erected at Diamond Wharf, and here all the guns

are landed, but the water is shoal and as the large lighters
cannot get up they must always be put into troop or paddle-box
boats. Shells and powder are also landed here, and hay and
chopped straw close to it.[5]

He then detailed the landing responsibilities and the
availability of manpower to do harbour improvements and
assist the movement of larger vessels:

A boarding book is kept from which the length of time a
vessel has been in harbour can be ascertained. There is a
tendency amongst the private traders to turn their ships into
retail shops, and to prevent this, notice should be given to them
on arriving that they will not be allowed to remain in harbour
beyond a certain day.

On the arrival of such a vessel her Master is required to sign a
notice that the sale of spirits or wine except to Officers is
forbidden, also a notice enjoining the utmost caution against
fire; also a notice to colliers forbidding the sale of coal; and one to
steamers requiring them to land all cinders on the beach to
harden the roads.

Every vessel on arriving should immediately send its invoices
of cargo to the department to which they are consigned, and will
receive thence directions for their disposal. The Commissary-
General receives the Commissariat goods. Mr Young, Commis-
sary of Ordnance, the ordnance stores; and Major Mackenzie,
DAQMG, the Quartermaster-General's stores.[6]

Heath was an excellent organiser and, as naval officers
often are, an inspired improviser. Thanks to him, the
movement of ships and the control of vessels in the harbour
improved materially even in the dead of winter: despite the
difficulties of entry into the inlet and the inadequacy of the
port as an advance base. He did his best too to dispose of
the flotsam, tow the carcases and corpses out to sea, and
rid the water of its worst accumulations. But there his
powers ended. Stores shipped from England, or trans-
shipped at Constantinople, and their management once un-

loaded in Balaclava were not his business but – in the main
– the Commissariat's.

But Mr Filder was also doing his best. With certain
exceptions, such as fuel and forage, the worst of the
deficiencies were made good by late 1854 or early 1855.
Food, clothing, medical supplies, non-war-like stores of all
kinds, even tents and huts, were assembling in gigantic
quantities at the waterside; guns and ammunition – the
business of the Ordnance Department – no less. The problem always was to get them up to the front. As early as
October 1854 the Commissariat had tried to

> . . . form depots of food, corn and forage, as a kind of reserve
> at the headquarters of the different divisions, but . . . their
> carts, arabas, wagons and horses were . . . taken for the use of
> the siege operations, and were employed in carrying shot, shell,
> ammunition, etc., to the trenches.[7]

In the event it was found impossible to put the plan into
operation until the following spring, since in the meantime
the winter storms had destroyed the surface of the track.
Traffic almost ceased. George wrote home repeatedly in the
sense that 'the roadside is lined with broken-down carts,
dead horses, mules, and men'; and Russell reported that

> . . . the Commissariat consumes and uses up horse-flesh at
> the rate of 100 head per week, and each of these animals costs
> an average of £5. The araba drivers from Roumelia and Bulgaria
> have disappeared likewise – out of the several hundreds there
> are now very few left.[8]

When horses and mules failed, men had to take their
place, and at one time half the survivors were taking it in
turns fetching and carrying for themselves and the other
half. The siege as such came for long periods to a halt. The
fearful difficulty of communication was ultimately overcome by the construction of a railway. On 29th December
Heath was advising the engineer where to lay the terminal

track, and by early February the navvies had begun work. By the time the system was in full working order, spring had come, the mud had dried and the track up to and around the camp was partially usable again. By then, too, many other things had improved. The worst of the winter and the worst confusion occurred between mid-November and early February, yet it was during this same period that the seeds of improvement were being sown. By the middle of February there was real evidence of progress. The weather had softened, hutting was going up, the railway had made a start, men were beginning to swear again, and even Russell admitted that things were on the mend. Moreover, public anger at the muddle and miseries of the winter had begun to take effect. On 1st February the Government fell. Lord Aberdeen was succeeded by Lord Palmerston as Prime Minister, and a new series of Commissions began to arrive, to enquire into the doings of every department. One manned by Sir John McNeill and Colonel Alexander Tulloch was concerned with 'The Supplies of the British Army in the Crimea' and was directed to investigate the Commissariat.

The two Commissioners left London on 23rd February and arrived at Constantinople on 6th March. They proceeded at once to Scutari, where they ascertained that the sick arriving from the Crimea were nearly all suffering from deficiency diseases, and that

. . . the food supplied to the army during the winter, consisting principally of salt meat and biscuit, with a very insufficient proportion of vegetables, were calculated . . . to produce those diseases.[9]

They arrived at Balaclava on 12th March, called on Lord Raglan, and with his authority started to examine all the commanders and their staffs down to brigade, together with their medical and commissariat officers; also the Quarter-

master-General and his senior assistants, and the Commissary-General and his. The examinations, both verbal and
written, gave birth ultimately to two reports. The first,
dated June 1855, related mainly to the Commissariat. The
second, dated January 1856, dealt with the Quartermaster-
General's Department, the Medical Department, and
Commissariat book-keeping. Both reports were backed by
a thick wad of printed evidence, statistical tables, and other
appendices.

The Commissioners were presented with 'a remarkable
concurrence of testimony as to matters of fact'. Everyone
agreed that most of the sickness and mortality derived from
overwork, exposure, improper food, and insufficient clothing and shelter; and that the origin of all these troubles lay
in the lack of transport. It was a convenient scapegoat; and
Mr Filder was able to say, without hesitation or fear of
contradiction, that the shortage of horses and mules was
dictated by the shortage of forage. Without sufficient hay
or chopped straw, it had proved impossible in the bad
months to maintain supplies to the forward troops. The
next question was obvious, and Mr Filder was ready for it.

. . . when there was full expectation of the army advancing
to the Danube, I made a contract for about 3,500 tons of hay,
to be delivered loose at different places in the neighbourhood of
Constantinople; and I also desired the Commissariat officer
there to form a depot of chopped straw, in case the army should
return and occupy cantonments in Turkey during the winter.
Subsequently, when it became known that we were to proceed
to the Crimea, the contractors, at my request, were willing to
engage to deliver about 500 tons of the hay pressed instead of
loose; but learning, in the early part of September, when the
army was on the way to the Crimea, that I could not rely on the
fulfilment of this contract, I wrote to England, requesting that
2,000 tons of hay might be sent from thence. Of this demand
only about one-tenth was forwarded, and that portion reached

Balaclava on 30th November. . . . The consignments fell greatly
short of my wants, the whole of the quantities forwarded from
England during a period of six months not amounting to the
2,000 tons for which I first made a requisition for about two
months' supply.

No exertion on the part of the Commissariat could remedy the
deficiency, it being impracticable to convey across the Black Sea
chopped straw or hay loose in sufficient quantities, or to procure
the means of pressing enough of either for the consumption of a
large army.[10]

The Commissioners were not satisfied, however. Why had
Mr Filder not seen to it that the 3,500 tons of hay collected
at Constantinople were shipped forward at once? The
answer: because some of the contractors, being small men,
had defaulted in delivery; because, owing to a mistake on
the part of the local Commissariat officer, the hydraulic
presses sent out from England for compressing the hay and
chopped straw into bales had been set up in the wrong place,
i.e. about fifteen miles from the main forage depots; and
because it had been difficult to procure the necessary shipping across the Black Sea.

Here lay the kernel of the catastrophe. Forage was the
controlling factor; but forage was not an operational matter
requiring the attention of the Chief-of-Staff, but merely a
Commissariat chore. Let Filder get on with it. But Mr
Filder, being a civilian, had no standing in the senior
counsels of the Army; and although Lord Raglan himself
had been sympathetic at a late stage and helped in some
degree, he did not grasp the full gravity of the situation
until after the November hurricane. For his part, Mr Filder
had neither the initiative nor the drive to surmount the
crisis by dynamic action. It was too much to expect from
an old man who had stuck to the rules all his life, had last
seen action in the Peninsular War, and against his will had
been dug out of the depths of Ireland for this one. On the

contrary, he fell back on the security of the regulations, and no one could fault him there.[11]

This is what the Commissioners discovered, for the regulations themselves were far more at fault than Mr Filder. When the troops were so sickened by the salt rations, that they preferred to go hungry, nothing was done to make a regular issue of alternative foods actually in store, such as rice, preserved vegetables and barley. Why? Because meat and biscuit were a standard issue, while vegetables – according to the regulations – had to be bought by the soldiers themselves in the open market; but there were no markets in the winter of 1854–5 in the Crimea. When men with sore gums from scurvy could no longer eat biscuit, no official action was taken to bake soft bread in the Russian ovens found in Balaclava, although there was flour in store. Why? Because a floating steam bakery had been promised from home. It did not arrive, however, until 12th May 1855; meanwhile, private enterprise supplied the need, 'and the men, especially the sick, eagerly purchased the loaf of the nominal weight of two pounds, at two shillings, and even at two shillings and sixpence or three shillings'.[12] After the countryside round Sebastopol had been denuded of wood, and men were reduced to grubbing for roots in the frozen ground, no fuel was issued, not even for cooking. Why? Because the regulations laid down that fuel might only be issued to troops in barracks, not to those in the field. Ultimately charcoal was made available. Officers got most of it, and at least one of them died of asphyxiation in his tent.

And so the sad story continued – fresh meat and vegetables, farinaceous foods, lime-juice, tea, coffee, porter: the Commissariat had them all; but either they could not be conveyed to the troops or the regulations prevented their being issued at all. The Commissioners remarked:

It seems to be a defect in the system of the British Army, that no one is specially responsible for the fitness of the diet supplied to the troops. . . . Supplies of the utmost value to health may be lying within reach, without being made available, because they are not specified in the scale of rations, and because there is no one whose especial duty it is to find them out and to suggest their employment. . . . It may be worthy of consideration whether there ought not to be upon the staff of an army in the field an officer, holding high military rank, whose duty it should be to devote his attention to the supply of the army, who should be responsible for everything connected with the receipt and issue of supplies and stores of every description, in the same manner as the Quartermaster-General and the Adjutant-General. . . .[13]

The Quartermaster-General had even less excuse than Mr Filder for the deficiencies of his department, for he at least was a military officer of high rank. Moreover, as Mr Filder pointed out, the Commissariat acted only as store-keeper for the QMG, and made issues solely on his requisition; and on him rested responsibility for all matters pertaining to clothing and equipment.[14] Indeed the QMG's department in England and the Crimea had much to answer for. There were numerous complaints of poor quality. The boots, not always available in the right sizes, leaked readily and the soles often came off after a few days. The clothing was spongy in texture, badly put together, and quite unfit to stand the wear and tear of the rough work of the trenches: the result, thought the Commissioners, of placing Army contracts with the lowest bidders.

Worse still, despite the critical losses due to the sinking of the *Prince*, Balaclava was bursting with coatees, trousers, greatcoats, underclothing, boots, rugs and blankets, at least by mid-December; yet little reached the shivering troops until well into the following year. It was the old story. Either regulations forbade the issue – of greatcoats, for instance, more than once in three years; or the transport was not available; or the quartermasters with the troops were simply not told that the goods had arrived. What worried the issuing officers most was the reconciliation of returns. Despite endless paper work, discrepancies between quantities taken into store and actual issues built up into thousands, and no one could account for them. The Commissioners never solved the puzzle. They dismissed corruption as the cause, since the scale was too great; but concluded it all arose out of the different procedures in use, and from the fact that discrepant quantities turned up now and again in some forgotten shed in Balaclava port. Probably also excessive precautions introduced in the eighteenth century to prevent peculation played their part; for they involved a whole series of signatures and counter-signatures by senior officers before the smallest issue could be made.

Russell commented:

We are cursed by a system of 'requisitions', 'orders', and 'memos', which is enough to depress an army of scriveners, and our captains, theoretically, have almost as much work to do with pen and paper as if they were special correspondents or bankers' clerks.[15]

By the time the Supplies Commissioners had published their first report, the new Government was already busy with Army reforms. In March 1855 the first steps were being taken to form the Land Transport Corps, so long demanded by Lord Raglan, a military corps independent of the Commissariat, hitherto responsible for transport. The Commissariat itself was transferred from the Treasury to the War Office, but retained its civilian status. These were panic measures, since from now on

. . . there was one authority in charge of the waggon and another in charge of the load, which was unsound in principle; and, worse than that, the setting of supply upon a civil and

FRENCH AMBULANCE, BEFORE SEBASTOPOL.

WASHING ESTABLISHMENT FOR THE GENERAL HOSPITAL AT BALACLAVA.

transport upon a military basis, tended to make the transport service give itself the airs of a combatant corps, thus widening the breach between the two services which should have been from the first united into one.[16]

Not until 1888 were supply and transport reunited, this time under the wholly military auspices of the Army Service Corps. Meantime, in the 1870s, the Army underwent a series of radical reforms under the direction of Edward Cardwell, Secretary of State for War, who secured supreme Parliamentary authority over all military affairs. The purchase of commissions was abolished, a Short Service Act was introduced, and henceforward regiments were raised on a local basis. But it took twenty years to bring this about, and then in the face of determined opposition; while even more remained to be done in the sphere of staff training and in the reorganisation of medical and hospital services.

K

13 : Whose fault was it –
the Medical Department's?

It had been Russell's reports about the medical mishandling of Alma, and the absence of proper nursing in the hospitals, that had first fired public indignation, stirred *The Times* on 13th October 1854 to open a Patriotic Fund for the purchase of comforts for the sick and wounded, and provoked the Government into appointing a Commission[1] to investigate 'the state of the hospitals of the British Army in the Crimea and Scutari'. Meanwhile, although Florence Nightingale had made her own arrangements to sail for Constantinople with a party of nurses, Russell's dispatch prompted Sidney Herbert, Secretary at War, to send her under his official aegis: a move calculated both to strengthen her authority in Turkey and attribute credit to the Government for prompt action.

The Hospitals Commission consisted of a barrister, Mr Benson Maxwell, and two doctors, Dr Cumming and Dr Spence, the latter subsequently losing his life on the *Prince*. The Commissioners started their enquiry towards the end of November and finally rendered their Report in February 1855, by which time – as noted – the situation in the Crimea was beginning to improve. The Report was a penetrating document, and dealt in great detail with four main and connected subjects:

The transport of wounded, and of medicines and medical equipment in the field.

The accommodation provided by field hospitals, together with their staffing and equipment.

The treatment of sick and wounded on board ship between the Crimea and Turkey.

The state of the hospitals at Scutari (a subject outside the province of this book).

The Commission examined a very large number of military and medical officers and other persons, and published their statements, together with a summary and several tables of statistics. Its recommendations were self-revealing and conformed to the general consensus of opinion at the front, reinforcing George Lawson's experiences from the landing at Calamita Bay until the onset of winter before Sebastopol.

Under the first heading it recommended that every regiment should have one or two light vehicles (of the jaunting-car type) to carry wounded and others who fell out on the march; that a proper ambulance corps be formed of fit and trained men (including farriers, wheelwrights and other tradesmen), equipped with newly-designed ambulances and other waggons for transporting medical and culinary stores; finally, that 'a body of mules, equipped like the mules of the French ambulance, should be formed, as an auxiliary to the ambulance waggons', to carry sick and slightly wounded over country where waggons could not go.

Under the second heading it recommended that every regiment should have a permanent supply of hospital accommodation and furniture (not bell-tents, which had proved unsuitable), and at least a fortnight's supply of medicines, with a three-month reserve at division or further back; that the system of requisition be overhauled; that the men be regularly inspected by the medical officer, especially those returning from trench or picket duty in winter; that

the medical NCOs and orderlies be better paid; and that
serious cases of illness be sent back to base.

The General Hospital at Balaclava was then considered
in detail. Formerly the village school, it consisted of

> . . . two parallel ranges of buildings about forty feet apart,
> situated on the side of a hill. . . . There are two smaller buildings,
> one roofless and both in bad repair, at right angles to these, but
> not connected with either, one of which is allotted to the medical
> officers for their quarters and for the purveyor's stores, while the
> other is occupied as a pack store. The school-rooms, three in
> number, are in good repair . . . and are heated by stoves of
> Russian construction. . . . Two marquees stood in front of the
> hospital; and [in January 1855] four wooden huts were in the
> course of erection.[2]

At 700 cubic feet per patient, excluding the huts, the
maximum accommodation was estimated to be 110 beds.
In fact, the number veered regularly between 200 and 300,
and in October 1854 topped 500. Even so, every man had a
bedstead and a palliasse, and an ample supply of blankets
and rugs, but no sheets. The means of ablution consisted of
one portable bath (occupied by a French soldier when the
Commission visited Balaclava); the cooking arrangements
were barely adequate; the laundry was conducted 'not
very effectually'; while the privies were considered 'very
bad'.

> The smell from the drains is offensive, and has been . . . the
> cause of fever and bowel complaints among several surgeons who
> lived in the immediate vicinity.[2]

Yet, in the circumstances, the Hospital passed muster. It
never compared in horror to Scutari, and neither satisfied
nor entirely horrified anyone. It was criticised by the
Sanitary Commission,[3] and it displeased Florence Nightingale when she visited Balaclava in May 1855, but her
impressions on that occasion were coloured by her feud with

Dr John Hall and by the hostility of Mrs Elizabeth Davis, the fiery Welsh cook in command of the Hospital kitchen. In any event, the main difficulty at Balaclava was that the Hospital authorities were overstraining their resources by trying to serve two purposes simultaneously: to treat men whose condition did not justify their transfer to Scutari, and to act now and then as a transit camp by taking in cases that reached the harbour too late in the day for embarkation; but that was part of another, more scandalous story, considered under the third heading of the Commission Report.

In this section the Commissioners criticised the absence of proper hospital ships[4] to convey the wounded after the Battle of the Alma to Scutari, and all the confusion, misery and mortality it occasioned – past history, it was true, but what steps had since been taken to put matters right?

Shortly after the arrival of the Army before Sebastopol, the Principal Medical Officer at Balaclava was charged with the duty of inspecting vessels destined for the transport of the sick and wounded.

On the 12th of December a General Order directed that this duty should in future be performed by a Board consisting of the Commandant of Balaclava, the DAQMG doing duty at that place, the Principal Medical Officer there, and an Assistant Commissary-General, in the presence of the Transport Agent or his deputy. With the exception of the addition of the last-mentioned member, this Board is constituted in conformity with the regulations of the service.

These gentlemen ... in estimating the number of patients which a vessel can properly carry, allow 6 feet by $2\frac{1}{2}$ feet for sick, and 6 feet by 3 feet for wounded men.[5]

The Commissioners considered the allowance too small, and then issued a long questionnaire concerning embarkation, conditions on board ship, and the voyage itself; and

from the replies received they composed a table[6] showing
as nearly as possible what happened on each ship carrying
sick and wounded between the Crimea and Scutari between
15th September 1854 and 13th February 1855. The table
revealed some very bad cases of overcrowding, gross inefficiency at all stages, and appalling misery in consequence.

In September out of 430 men loaded on to the *Caduceus*
114 died in six days, the majority of them suffering from
Asiatic cholera. This was a 'record', but the rate of mortality
continued high right into January, when, for example, 47
out of 177 died on the *Shooting Star*. Little of this was due
to deliberate neglect. Surgeons and orderlies (the majority
untrained and nominally subject to military, not medical,
authority) were so hard pressed that dressings might be
left unchanged for days on end, and maggots appear in the
wounds. Urinals, bed-pans and ordinary lavatory accommodation never seemed sufficient, so that – when dysentery
was raging – a great quantity of bedding had to be destroyed. Cooking too was poorly done, and diet often totally
unsuitable for sick soldiers. One of the worst aspects was
the manner of embarkation and the delay before sailing. In
early days patients brought down from the camp were
simply dumped beside the landing-stage at the head of the
inlet, put into open boats and then rowed out to the allotted
ships. Theoretically, the whole operation was in the hands
of the PMO of the port, assisted by a naval officer. At
best it was a slow and tedious performance, but made
far worse when the men arrived at Balaclava without
notice.

We think . . . that the practice of sending down to the harbour
from 600 to 1,200 men together for embarkation, has endangered
the lives of many, in wet weather, from the long exposure on the
beach to which they were subjected. They ought to be sent in
much smaller detachments, so that the whole number in each
detachment might be taken on board at once.[7]

In time the procedure was improved. An officer from the QMG's department was detailed to accompany the men down to the harbour, a canvas shelter (mentioned by Captain Heath)[8] was erected on the wharf, and by the General Order of 12th December the ships were officially inspected before sailing.

However, there was no knowing if a ship was always available, or when it would sail. The *Medway* started taking men on board on 7th November, but did not leave harbour for three weeks, finally arriving at Scutari on the 24th. In the end action was taken to convert four vessels into something like real hospital ships, having a permanent medical staff attached: with the result that the *Melbourne* made the journey in February 1855 with the loss of only two men out of 170 sick, and the *Brandon* with one out of 118.

The Commission did not accuse anyone of criminal incompetence, but made it clear how a host of individuals had become entangled in the toils of an antediluvian system which no one, it seemed, had the power to reform or replace. Incompetence, in fact, was built into the system, or multiplicity of systems; and the only hope of solution lay in a General Staff composed of officers, trained in the whole field of operations and administration, and serving a commander who had himself had staff experience. But that was a dream to remain unrealised for fifty years.

A really ruthless commander might possibly have imposed order in the Crimea itself; but Raglan was not ruthless. As he and his staff were out of touch with the problems of administration, he reacted as a rule in agonised silence to all the muddle and suffering around him, and resented all the more deeply the reports that were reaching the public. For that reason he blew hot and cold towards the Medical Department. He never understood why they could not cope. In his despatch after Inkerman he praised the PMOs of the Divisions by name, and added that

> . . . the arrangements of the Inspector-General of Hospitals, Dr Hall, for the care of the wounded, merit the expression of my entire approbation.

However, after the hurricane, his mood changed, and in a General Order dated 13th December concerning conditions on board the steamship *Avon*, he publicly deplored the lack of medical attention and ordered that the PMO at Balaclava be relieved of his post. Moreover, he felt

> . . . unable to exonerate Dr Hall from all blame in this matter, as it was his duty, either by personal inspection or by the reports of his subordinates, to have ascertained that the ship was furnished with everything necessary for the comfort of the many sick and wounded on board, which the public service could by any possibility afford.

The *Avon* was certainly a bad case, but by no means the worst. Naturally enough, without denying its seriousness, Dr Hall saw the matter in a different light and he took strong objection to the way in which the enquiry was conducted. His diary[9] tells the tale.

Dec 1: About 12 last night the Adjutant-General came to my tent with an angry letter from Lord Raglan, stating that an officer of rank had told him about a poor wounded man who had lost both his legs was lying on the deck of the *Avon* with only a blanket on him. He directed the A-Genl and me to go and investigate the matter, and he said if there was neglect he would bring the offenders to a court martial. This morning we went down in a torrent of rain and went on board the *Avon*. The poor man was fretful from pain, having got Hospital Gangrene of the stump. . . . Today he had a mattress under him and every attention appeared to have been paid to him and he was judiciously placed near the gangway for the benefit of fresh air – but his case is hopeless – he is in great pain and fretful. The ship is not in very good order and ports were all closed on account of the weather, which occasioned a bad smell in some of the small cabins where attention had not been paid to the emptying of the slop pails. There are 297 sick on board, 22 of whom are wounded and 275 cases of rheumatism, frost bite of the toes, and bowel complaints. There are three medical officers on board – Asst-Surgeon Wilson 11th Hussars, 6 years' standing; Mills 60th Regt, 6 months' standing; Staff Asst-Surgeon Reade, 9 months. Mr Wilson had been confined to his bed for two days but will be fit for duty again tomorrow. Mr Mills has a sore on his leg but was at duty today, and it was reported by Col. Davis to Lord Raglan that there was only one medical man on board! His Lordship is still angry about the newspaper reports and says he must have the matter investigated by a Court of Enquiry! ! ! !

The Court was duly held and the General Order blaming the Medical Department published. But the public was never told that, although medical matters were primarily at stake, the Court was entirely composed of military officers. Neither Hall nor Dr Robert Lawson, the PMO at Balaclava (no relation of George), was given a copy of the evidence. Lawson was examined as a witness, unaware that he was being arraigned for dereliction of duty: the ironic fact being that he had not been PMO when the *Avon* was inspected prior to embarkation. This duty had been carried out by his predecessor, Dr Tice, a senior medical officer, who had attested the ship's stores for a voyage of thirty-six hours and passed her for a complement of 350. There was no reason – in the context of the conditions then prevailing – to assume he had been wrong. *But the ship did not sail for a fortnight,* and nothing was done apparently to replenish the stores, or ensure that in every other respect the ship was as ready as it had been at the outset. The real trouble was that responsibility was divided, although the PMO had

to bear the blame; and it was this case that caused the
General Order to be published on 12th December, directing
that a Board of officers from different departments inspect
each ship before sailing, and so take collective responsibility.[10]

The fact that Dr Robert Lawson was a namesake of
George caused him some embarrassment;[11] but, more than
that, the handling of the whole incident aroused in him a
deep resentment against Lord Raglan. He wrote to his
mother on 17th December:

You will, probably before this reaches you, have seen in *The
Times* a very severe General Order from Lord Raglan against the
Medical Department in which he particularly names a Dr
Lawson for neglect of duty etc., etc. Now this individual is not
myself, but a Staff Surgeon who was Principal Medical Officer
in Balaclava, one of the best officers, I am told, in the service,
unjustly abused by Lord Raglan who is anxious, I have no doubt,
to throw on the Medical Department the blame due to the
military authorities for not having those requisites placed on
board ship which are essential for the comfort of the sick troops.
The apathy which he complains of in Dr Lawson is the very
complaint laid against him by all here, for looking after his own
individual comforts and not caring much for the good of others
in the Field. Very seldom do we see anything of him in or near
camp, and I do not think that anyone here will often catch him
out in the wet. He is very bitter against our Department, and
you have I daresay noticed that in his despatches after an
action not one word of thanks does he give to the Doctors, who
really with very inefficient means work very hard, particularly
lately during the severe attack of cholera we have had in
camp.

Again, on 4th January 1855:

Lord Raglan called at our tent last night accompanied with
his Staff, to inquire about the sick. This, I think, is about the
second or third time he has made his appearance in our camp,

since the first two days of the siege. I think the old gentleman is beginning to feel alarmed about the state of the sick list. We had this morng 920 sick in *our* Division alone, and I think some of the Divisions have more, not taking into account the number already sent away and sick in hospital at Scutari. He seemed ignorant as to what was the real state of affairs, and surprised when we told him that we knew there was everything in Balaclava, but want of transport prevent our bringing up the absolute necessaries to camp.

On 12th January to his brother Fred:

Lord Raglan has at last, and in inclement weather too, made his appearance in and about camp, brought out from his house, I expect, by a letter written by our Principal Medical Officer of the Division, Dr Pine,[12] in which he stated to Sir R. England[13] (for the information of Lord Raglan) that the immense amount of sickness in the Division depended on the men being half starved, ill clad, and over worked, and that the Medical Officers were unable to bring up stores sufficient for the sick, or huts, or marquees to cover them, owing to no aid in the way of transport being given by either the Commissariat or Quarter-master-General's Department. Such being the subject of the letter his Lordship came down to camp to see Dr Pine, and was very indignant at such wholesome truths being told him, and left in rather a pet ordering the matter to be enquired into. . . . Suffice it to say . . . that his Lordship has since called at our tents to see Dr Pine, was most condescending in his manner, and hoped that he would ask for whatever he wanted for the sick, and that if it were possible he would have it immediately.

And on 15th January to his brother Willie:

You are in your letter indignant, and I think justly, at Russell, *The Times* correspondent, saying that England does not care one straw for those in the Crimea. This is of course a statement every-one here knows to be incorrect, but as far as I have read of what you call the dismal news in *The Times*, there is not one syllable but what is perfectly true, and not in the least degree exaggerated. With regard to what *The Times* has stated concerning Lord Raglan, it is also true. Up to within the last week or ten days he has been, as far as the troops are concerned, almost invisible, staying quietly at a very comfortable house at Headquarters about 2 miles from this camp and not knowing – and everyone here will go so far as to say – not caring as to what condition the troops are in. Latterly he has, as I told you in my last letter, made more frequent visits to camp, and did not relish the truth of the condition of the men being told him at first. He has however now become more condescending and gracious in his manner, and is doing all, I firmly believe, now in his power to ameliorate the state of the sick.

In his book, *The Destruction of Lord Raglan*,[14] Christopher Hibbert has divined the truth about Lord Raglan's character. It was his very qualities of sensitivity, reticence and aristocratic reserve – expressed, for example, in his aversion to wearing a uniform or to any kind of public display – that made it seem he did not care. In essence, George Lawson's comments were about as deserved and undeserved as those published against the Medical Department, wherein all the appearances, and some of the reality, testified against both parties. Under severe stress, even the most fair-minded of men gave way to bitter accusation in the Crimea.

The Hospitals Commission was the first of an apparently endless series of bodies set up to enquire into the medical business of the Army. Whereas this Commission had originally been suggested by the Director-General of the Army Medical Department, most of those that followed were initiated by Lord Panmure, the new Secretary of State for War; or by J. A. Roebuck, Radical MP for Sheffield, whose attack on the conduct of the campaign had brought down the previous administration. The very profusion of committees and commissions, the haste

attaching to their appointment, and the background of
Press prejudice and provocation were symptoms of the
nation's guilty conscience. Finding fault often seemed the
chief purpose, rather than any genuine desire to pursue
enquiries and secure reforms; but not all the investigators were so minded, and even those who at first exerted
every effort to pin the entire blame on to a handful of
officials were perceptibly influenced by the sifting-out
of the truth.

Two delegations – the Supplies Commission and the Sanitary Commission – were sent out at once, and began work
early in March 1855.

The activities of the Supplies Commission (Tulloch and
McNeill) have already been related in the previous chapter;
but in their second report the Commissioners included some
paragraphs on medical matters, including a direct criticism
of Dr Hall. They commented on the shortage of medicines,
equipment and comforts during the winter months, and
found it strange that the medical officers at the front could
not extract these things from the stores in Balaclava. Dr
Hall protested that the base depot at Scutari had failed to
comply with his requisitions; whereupon the Commissioners
felt bound to say

. . . that at a time when the existence of a great portion of the
sick was imperilled by the absence of these supplies, something
more than the mere transmission of the usual official demand on
the Purveyor or the Apothecary at Scutari was necessary. . . .
A proper officer might have been sent to Scutari, with instructions to bring back whatever was most urgently required for
the hospitals.[15]

The Sanitary Commission consisted of Mr Robert Rawlin-
son, a civil engineer, Dr John Sutherland of the Board of
Health, and Dr Hector Gavin; and was accompanied by a
party of officials from the Borough of Liverpool, then in the

forefront of public health administration. The Commission
was instructed to investigate the sanitary condition of
hospital buildings and camps in Turkey and the Crimea,
and see that things got done.

It is important that you be deeply impressed with the
necessity of not resting content with an order, but that you
see instantly, by yourselves or your agents, to the commencement of the work and to its superintendence day by day until
it is finished.[16]

In its preliminary report to the Cabinet dated 16th April,
the Commission commented mainly on the hospitals at
Scutari and Kulali, and on two hospital ships lying off
Seraglio Point. In the Crimea, however, an immediate
difficulty arose. Dr Gavin, who had been deputed to go to
Balaclava, died in a pistol accident in April; while otherwise
the Commission had some difficulty in penetrating the
defences erected by Dr Hall.[17] None the less it carried out
its instructions; for there was no doubt that, despite the
devotion to duty of Dr Anderson and his staff, there was
still a great deal wrong with the state of Balaclava in the
spring of 1855. As Florence Nightingale herself pointed
out:

The British Army took ground before Sebastopol at the end
of September 1854. There is no record of any preliminary proceeding having taken place on that occasion. No survey, no
topographical report, no sanitary report, no cautions to military
authorities, no sanitary memoranda to medical officers of
divisions. . . . No sanitary measures were organized for securing
the health of Balaclava, the very basis of operations.[18]

Medical officers had not been trained in sanitary routine
– often they were so busy dealing with the sick and wounded
that they had no time to think of anything else – and there
seemed to be no overall authority responsible for, or capable

of enforcing, sanitary precautions in the port or the camps. Ordinary standards of behaviour, especially among the Turks, were so low that the mere summary of what the Sanitary Commission did do speaks for itself:

The graveyard [at the head of the inlet], and all the filth that could not be burnt, were covered over with lime, charcoal and earth. Latrines were erected; a cleansing staff was organized; a Russian barge, which had been blown out of the harbour of Sebastopol, was employed at Balaclava in carrying such refuse out to sea as could not be burnt on shore; a slaughtering place was provided; houses were lime-washed inside and out; the shoal water at the head of the harbour filled up; the decaying matter along the east side of the harbour deodorized, and covered in with, temporary quays. Drains were made; one of the sources of water supply was covered over. Three Naval Surgeons daily made an inspection of the ships; cleansed, lime-washed, fumigated, ventilated, or removed the ships out of harbour. Dead animals were towed out to sea. The worst houses were pulled down. These works advanced slowly, from the deficiency of labour; but, by the end of July, they were so far advanced that the Commandant could carry them on alone – and Balaclava became, what it might have been from the beginning, as healthy a little seaport as can be seen.

As to the camps on the Heights:

Comparatively little had here to be done by the Sanitary Commission, and that chiefly in the construction of huts. . . . The camps of the Guards before Sebastopol, and of the Highland Brigade beyond Kamara, became sanitary models. Little fault can be found with the arrangements of the second winter (1855–6).[19]

The Sanitary Commission finally published its report in March 1857, and showed it was concerned less with personalities than with practical action; even so, it generated a lively interchange between Dr Sutherland and Dr Hall. Its findings were in the main absorbed by the Royal Commission[20] appointed in May with Sidney Herbert in the chair: a move managed by Florence Nightingale, lately returned from the Crimea, and who was determined to devote the rest of her life to reforming military medical organisation as a whole.

Dr Andrew Smith was a member of this latest Commission – he could hardly be left out – and at the same time its most important witness, giving prolonged evidence before it, as he had done at two earlier Parliamentary enquiries into the work of the Army Medical Department.

In 1855, on the motion of Mr Roebuck, a Select Committee had been appointed –

. . . to enquire into the condition of our Army before Sebastopol and into the conduct of those Departments of the Government whose duty it has been to minister to the wants of the Army.

This was the 'Sebastopol Committee',[21] which sat all through March and was chaired by Roebuck himself. Far from wilting before a hostile inquisition, Dr Smith doggedly revealed the size and complexity of the problems he had to face. It soon became clear that, while responsible to a multitude of overlapping authorities, his own powers and resources were absurdly limited. All he could do – and had done – was to order the necessary stores and send out the requisite staff.[22] What happened in Turkey and the Crimea was in the hands of the men on the spot. He could only advise and react on information received – if he was allowed to receive it, for even the Hospitals Commission (which had been his own idea) was not allowed to report to him direct. Fortunately, he was as methodical as he was persistent. He had carefully filed all his correspondence with the War Office since the day he took over the Department; and it was the publication of these letters that helped ensure his ultimate vindication.[23]

Ships in Balaclava Harbour

Commissariat difficulties. The road from Balaclava to Sebastopol, at Kadikoi

A year later, in May 1856 and six weeks after the end of the war, he was examined for nearly three days by a second Select Committee,[24] under the chairmanship of Augustus Stafford, MP, who in a private capacity had visited Scutari at the worst time. Smith explained that, by agreement with the Government, considerable reorganisation had already taken place both in his own Department and in the field, where a new corps – The Medical Staff Corps – had been formed the previous June. The Corps, however, was having teething troubles; indeed, it proved a failure – like so many of the instant reforms rushed through by the new Government in 1855. Two years later it was replaced by the Army Hospital Corps, which provided orderlies in general and garrison hospitals and stretcher-bearers in the field, the men bearing Army ranks and having proper military status at last. But the Corps did not staff regimental hospitals, nor did it include officers; and it was not until 1873 that this anomaly was abolished.

Meanwhile, the foundations for general reform of the Army Medical Service had been laid by the Royal Commission of 1857–8. Its recommendations included the establishment of a medical school, the introduction of a statistical branch, improved barracks and hospitals, and better pay and conditions of service. Some of these measures were forced through in the ensuing decade; but it required the lessons of the Franco-Prussian War of 1870–1, and the Cardwell reforms that followed, to right most of the wrongs revealed by the Crimea almost twenty years before.[25]

Dr Andrew Smith retired in May 1858 and was awarded the KCB. He had done his duty well, although *The Times* did not think so; but posterity will agree he deserved the honour, for he had to bear responsibility for the errors of his predecessors, and in doing so he kept his head, leaving a detailed record of his term of office, without which the reformers could hardly have gone to work.

L

Dr John Hall retired in January 1857. He had already
received his KCB, and endured – and was to continue to
endure – the gibes of his critics. Posterity still finds it
difficult to be fair to Hall. He had had an impossible task
in the Crimea; but he was not the kind of man to overcome
impossibilities, having neither the stature, nor the initiative,
nor the social confidence to do so. He was a less attractive
victim of circumstances.

14 : Hell shrinks

LETTERS: 18th JANUARY – 25th MARCH 1855

The search for scapegoats was of no comfort or concern to George Lawson who was still serving on the Heights when conditions were at their worst. On 18th January 1855, however, he wrote:

I received an order yesterday at 2 o'clock in the afternoon to proceed at once to Balaclava, and report myself to the Senior Medical Officer there. I was at the time just starting off with sick to conduct them to this place to put them on board ship, having as usual to return again to camp as soon as I had discharged my duty. I had consequently no time to pack up my traps, but I told my servant to put all my luggage on my pack pony (which is a Russian) and follow me with them; and instead of returning I was told that I was to take charge of sick officers, who had been sent from camp to Balaclava for further treatment. Dr Anderson[1] is the Principal Medical Officer here, he attended me with Dr Forrest when I was ill. I am to take up my quarters in his house, and I have a small room to myself which opens into his, we shall thus have to mess together.

The house is a small one, very much like a little country cottage with whitewashed walls; we have tables, chairs, wardrobes, etc., in it. It is in just the same condition as when the last Russian gentleman who lived here left it; he went away of course in a hurry when we took possession of Balaclava, and not being able to carry his furniture with him we reap the benefit of his misfortunes. It is situated on the side of a hill, at

149

the extreme and best end of the town, and commands a view
of all the shipping in Balaclava. From my window I can see
every vessel which comes in or goes out of harbour.

I have thus you see again dropped on my legs. I am comfortably housed, and have a large Russian bedstead to sleep in.
Last night was the first night I have slept under a roof, with the
exception of once on the march, for about 7 months. You may
imagine I could not sleep much, and many times in the night
wished myself almost back again under canvas, cold and windy
as it was, but this I shall soon get over; and I am, and shall be
of course, far more comfortable here than I should be if I
remained in the snow in front of Sebastopol.

But he issued a warning:

I am here however only conditionally, and Dr Hall has told
Dr Anderson that, should my services be wanted in the front
again, I must go.

George soon saw how things were beginning to improve,
though very slowly at first. Warm clothing had already
arrived 'in enormous quantities', and 'a daily inspection of
the men is now ordered, to see that they really have the
warm clothing which has been issued to them'. Wooden
huts were also being delivered – but the difficulty of transport remained.

The roads still continue in very bad condition, almost
impassable to anything but baggage animals. The French are
now making roads for us, macadamizing them with the stone
which exists everywhere here in such great quantities; but it is a
very long job, and from the great traffic will require continual
working at. . . . A few of the huts have already been erected in
camp, and capital hospitals they form. Had they but arrived
a little sooner, much sickness and suffering would have been
spared the men.

The climate gave ground for hope too. When George first
settled in at Balaclava in the middle of January, 'some days

were fine overhead, but others nothing but severe north-
easterly winds, snow and sleet during the whole day'. Washing water still froze before he got to it, and his boots still
had to be thawed out before he could put them on. The last
week of January, however, brought a fine spell. Despite hard
frosts at night, the snow vanished and the sun shone most
of the day. The track to the camp dried out sufficiently for a
consignment of hutting and supplies to be rushed up to the
forward troops. Although the weather deteriorated again,
and proved as trying as ever for sheer waywardness,
spring was surely on its way, and in 1855 it would come
early. Life was becoming tolerable, even pleasant, for
George.

I am beginning to get now more reconciled to living in a
house, and enjoy sitting over a charcoal fire in a stove in the
centre of the room, reading the newspaper or some book which I
have borrowed. I begin to fancy myself a civilised being again.

On either side of the harbour of Balaclava are enormous hills
or rather mountains; and on the right, at the top of one of these
as you enter the harbour, is an old Genoese fort at an enormous
height from the sea. I walked up there yesterday, the sight is
really very fine, you look down upon the sea and those terrible
rocks, upon which the *Prince* and so many vessels were lost on
the 14th November: a day which will not, I think, be easily
forgotten by those who were in camp and experienced the discomfort produced by the gale. The whole surrounding country
from this spot presents a series of hills and ravines, which have
a very wild and beautiful appearance.

Hope, however, was still a tenuous thing. Men continued
to fall sick and die at a frightening rate. The 3rd, George's
own Division, had been reduced to 4,000 more or less fit
men.

You may imagine what must have been the sickness and
mortality in the army, when I tell you that the 63rd Regiment,

which came out here only in September and joined us when we
landed in the Crimea, is now numerically unfit for service. Its
strength is now only 65, besides 16 officers, and it came out I
believe 1,000.

A rumour of peace was rushing about – that the Czar had
'signed the four points required by the Western Powers' –
but no one really believed it.

I am afraid that Lord Raglan will have but a small army, out
of his original one, left in the spring. Vessels crowded with sick
are being sent away daily to Scutari, many are invalided home,
but few return again to the Crimea after they have been once
sent away.

Lord Raglan now pays frequent visits about camp, and comes
occasionally to Balaclava to look after the state of the Hospitals.
The brushing up he had in *The Times* has worked a good effect
on the old man. It is said that he frequently on his road speaks
to soldiers and asks them how they are. One day he asked,
'Well, my man, you have vegetables now, have you not?', 'Why,
yes, my lord, last week I had an onion which I bought at
Balaclava.' Another time, in civilian dress, he asked a private,
'Well, my man, you are well clothed now, are you not?' Upon
which the man opened his coat and revealed little but a rag
covering his skin. Lord Raglan then said, 'But you are well fed
now, are you not?' The man, not knowing who was speaking to
him, answered 'Now I see you be chaffing me,' and walked away
in disgust.

That peace was a rumour and no more was proved by the
renewal of preparations for the siege.

The guns have been brought up from Balaclava . . . and have
only now to be put in position in the new batteries. Shot and shell
are being carried up with as much rapidity as circumstances will
allow, principally by the French, and should this fine weather
continue we shall, I think, shortly again be able to open on the
Russians. The French are, I am told, ready and only waiting
for us. Sebastopol is now far stronger than ever; where batteries

have been destroyed, earthworks have been thrown up and
mounted with guns. They have indeed made good use of the
time we have given them and will, I am afraid, give a great
deal of trouble before the place is likely to fall.

While George was acclimatising himself to the relative
comforts of Balaclava, he encountered a college friend,
Douglas Reid, who had arrived at the port on 2nd February.[2] Reid had joined the service in October 1854 in
response to an appeal for 'acting assistant-surgeons' for
home service. In less than six weeks, however, he was
surprised to find himself gazetted to an Assistant-Surgeoncy
in the 90th Light Infantry in the Crimea. Balaclava was
not inviting.

It was a horrible night, bitterly cold and pouring with rain
when we entered the harbour and took up our position amongst
the scores of transports and miscellaneous craft with which it
was crowded. Nothing could be more depressing than the
outlook – dark, dismal, cheerless in the extreme. I did not leave
the *Clyde* that night; being advised that it was useless to expect
to find any one to whom I might report myself until the morning, and that to flounder about in the dark in the mud of
Balaclava was an unsafe proceeding for a newcomer.
Early the next morning I went on deck to have a look round.
The rain of the previous night was succeeded by a heavy fall
of snow, and a white world was revealed. The deck, the spars,
the ropes of the ship were covered with snow, as well as the hill
sides, and the buildings in Balaclava. The thermometer had
fallen to ten degrees below freezing point. I landed after breakfast, and found my way, after much wandering about, to the
Commandant's office, where I thought I ought to report myself.
The Commandant had gone out for a ride. I then went to seek
for the Principal Medical Officer, Dr Anderson, and was
fortunate enough to find him at his post. There I found also an
old college friend, George Lawson. He kindly accompanied me
to the Commissariat or Transport Office, where I tried to get a
baggage mule to convey my bullock trunks and bed to the

camp of the Light Division, eight miles distant. I was informed
that it was impossible to supply me with one that day, and as
it was equally impossible for me to get to the front without one,
there was nothing to do but wait and spend the rest of the day
in examining the town and making enquiries as to what was
going on at the front.

The 'town' . . . was a confused aggregation of wrecked houses,
a roofless church, huts of every description, stones, stables and
tents; and mud, dirt and slush everywhere. I was not sorry to
get back to the comforts of the ship again. . . . Soldiers were
hardly recognisable as such, their 'uniforms' being of a most
varied description. For instance, the Scots Greys were arrayed
in sailors' blue shirts, pea-jackets and helmets. Their chargers
were dying of starvation and overwork, many of them being
employed to drag boards to the front for the erection of the
hospital huts. It was said that the Turks were eating the flesh
of the dead horses and were glad to get it.

At last, on February 5th, I was provided with two pack mules
and a driver, and started for the front. My kit was strapped to
one – a bullock trunk on each side and the bedding in the middle
– and I was supposed to ride the other. . . . The track or road,
as it was called, was deep in mud and slush nearly all the way;
here and there on the higher ground it was possible to walk,
but for quite two-thirds of the distance, not being then provided
with ammunition boots, I had to ride, and I was truly thankful
when the journey came to an end.

When we reached the Woronzoff road I knew we had not much
farther to go, and as a matter of fact a few more yards brought
us to the 90th Camp, which was on the left of the Light Division.
Here two or three officers were strolling about. They stared at
me without giving me a friendly greeting, so it became necessary
for me to introduce myself, and ask the way to the Colonel's
quarters that I might report myself to him on joining the
regiment. They told me the Colonel was in the trenches, and
one of them kindly offered to take me there, which offer I was
glad to accept. Whether it was to test my valour . . . or because
it was a short cut, I cannot say; but instead of proceeding
through the covered way (i.e. a protected trench), he took me

across an open plateau, fully exposed to the Russian fire, and where shot and shell were flying about. Of these unpleasant missiles I took no notice outwardly, though inwardly I had nasty qualms, and I was considerably relieved when we reached Gordon's battery, where I found the Colonel, who gave me a kindly welcome.

After a few words I returned to camp by the same route (knowing no other) without damage. I then made the acquaintance of our surgeon, Dr R. C. Anderson,[3] who at my request took me to the 'hospital'. Naturally I expected to see a hut or building of some kind, and was much astonished when he pointed out a row of bell-tents pitched, like all the others, in the mud. I looked into some of them and found them crowded with sick, ten or twelve men in each tent with their feet towards the pole and their heads towards the curtain. They were lying on the bare ground wrapped in their great coats. It struck me that whatever was the matter with them they had a very poor chance of recovery. They were being sent down daily in batches to Balaclava for embarkation to Scutari or England. The diseases from which they suffered were chiefly dysentery and fever. The regiment had then been more than two months in camp, and this was the best they could do for their sick and wounded!

A walk round the camp revealed a very miserable state of things. Imagine a ploughed field after three days heavy rain followed by a snow storm, and you may be able to form some idea of the ground on which our tents were pitched; then imagine a cutting wind on an open plain and a temperature of 22 degrees F., no shelter of any kind except a canvas tent, not a house or a wall or a tree anywhere within sight, and you may picture the situation. Every tree and even the brushwood had been cut down and used for firewood long since. There had been vineyards, and they had also disappeared. But the roots remained in the ground, and parties of our men with much difficulty and labour grubbed them up for fuel. They often had to use pickaxes to get through the frozen ground before they could reach the roots, and it would take a fatigue party of six men a whole day to fill a small sack.

Reid, in short, found conditions no better than those which George Lawson had experienced during the worst of the winter. He messed with the other doctors in the senior surgeon's tent, and continued his comments:

The most important item was a table, made by a sailor. I mention it first, because it was an extraordinary luxury at the time; a box or a barrel generally did duty for a table. However, this one had four legs, and though small answered all our requirements. We had two camp stools, a potato basket and the mound round the tent pole as chairs. A deal box served as a cupboard and sideboard; a barrel also was made into another cupboard, the Doctor's bed became a sofa in the daytime, and there was a stove to warm the tent, dry our clothes and boil water.

With regard to food, we did not touch our rations of salt pork. It was quite enough to see the barrels of it opened and the great slabs of pork taken out. Between the layers there was a quantity of coarse salt. Sometimes there was an issue of what was called 'fresh meat', but it was seldom eatable, and the tinned meat was worse. Balaclava supplied us with goat mutton, very lean, at 2s a pound, and now and then we were able to buy a half-starved sheep or some poultry from the transports. No green vegetables could be obtained at any price. The coffee that was served out to us was in berry and unroasted. We had first to fry it in a frying-pan, and then grind it in the hollow of a 13-inch shell into which we fitted a round shot. By rolling the shot round and round, the coffee berries were broken up into a coarse powder. The process was tedious and not very satisfactory.

One of Reid's first duties was to accompany an officer, in an advanced stage of enteric fever, down to Balaclava. He was carried on a mule litter over the whole eight miles and – as Reid said – was only saved from the extremity of suffering by the fact that he was half-delirious. Fortunately, at the landing-stage at Balaclava, a boat was ready to take the case on board a 'hospital ship'; and there was a further surprise.

Here I made the acquaintance of a celebrated person, Mrs Seacole, a coloured woman, who out of the goodness of her heart and at her own expense, supplied hot tea to the poor sufferers while they were waiting to be lifted into the boats. I need not say how grateful they were for the warm and comforting beverage when they were benumbed with cold and exhausted by the long and trying journey from the front. . . . I saw my charge safely on board the ship and he lived to be taken into the hospital at Scutari, but died on February 24th. It is hard to say whether it was better to carry this officer away or to leave him where he was.

A few more words about Mrs Seacole. She did not spare herself if she could do any good to the suffering soldiers. In rain and snow, in storm and tempest, day after day she was at her self-chosen post, with her stove and kettle, in any shelter she could find, brewing tea for all who wanted it, and they were many. Sometimes more than 200 sick would be embarked on one day, but Mrs Seacole was always equal to the occasion.[4]

Reid resembled George Lawson in several ways, Both were doctors, practical and humane. They observed everything with the eye of common sense, and exercised a gift for understatement. As a regimental surgeon, Reid got closer to the enemy than George, but even on these occasions his dry humour did not desert him.

On reaching Gordon's battery, the 'Doctor's bunk' was pointed out to me. . . . It was constructed of balks of timber, sand bags, fascines, stones and earth, and was supposed to be bomb-proof. . . . When a heavy shot struck the parapet a tremor went through the whole structure, and, more or less, through the inmates.

It was also obvious that although things were getting tangibly better in Balaclava, at least by early February,

improvements were taking at least a month to reach the
front. On the 15th George complained that the quantity of
winter clothing reaching Balaclava was becoming embarras-
sing: 'I almost wish at times our over-anxious Government
had sent out summer clothing as well.' It was hard to know
how to deal with the Russian spring, which switched from
intense cold to oppressive warmth from one day to the next.
Reid recorded that in the early part of February spring
flowers were blooming in some of the ravines.

I picked a crocus on the field of Inkerman, and violets and
hyacinths were beginning to make a show. On the 21st . . . the
thermometer was two degrees below zero and the camp buried
in three feet of snow. It was difficult to get from one tent to
another; our men, many of them, were badly frost-bitten. . . .
While all this was going on we were told – and it turned out to
be true – that large quantities of warm clothing, both for
officers and men, were in the stores of the Commissariat department at Balaclava. All that arrived in our camp consisted of
eight short jackets lined with rabbit skin, and these were given
to senior officers. . . . Some young ladies sent us out from
England a supply of woollen cuffs or mits. These were very
comfortable. Some verses accompanied them. . . .

Later when the weather had reached a sustained heat and
the railway was working, heavy clothing was at last
emptied out of store and showered on the forward troops.
Reid said savagely:

The above instance of wicked mismanagement . . . reminds
me that March 21st was proclaimed, in the name of the Queen,
as a day of 'solemn fast, humiliation and prayer' throughout the
kingdom. The feeling in camp was that we had been sufficiently
humiliated already by the blunderings of the Government that
sent us out, without making proper provision for keeping us
alive afterwards. It would have been right enough for the
Government to prostrate themselves in dust and ashes, and

abase themselves for all their misdeeds, but why the people of England should be called upon to join them in this process of humiliation, when they were sacrificing all that was dear to them to save the country from disaster, no one could understand.

It seemed that every advance brought another blunder. George reported:

The Commissariat in their anxiety to give fresh meat to the troops have lately taken to have sheep killed at Constantinople and brought up here, in addition to the live cattle which they also get in small instalments for so many mouths. With the usual discretion and sense which have characterised most of the Crimean proceedings, these have either missed the vessel which ought to have brought them up here, or else have been kept too long before they were put on board and consequently have arrived in a state of extreme putrescence. Two days since two hundred sheep were condemned and buried, as being unfit for food, and today I saw many more consigned to the same fate. It is expected that our Commissary-General, Mr Filder, will – like all the other heads of departments – be made a KCB. Does this mean Knight of the Carrion Bullock, or Killer of Corrupt Beef?

On 17th February Consul Calvert[5] told George:

Whilst I hear on the one hand of the numerous wants of the Army, and of the scurvy having broken out among the men, I cannot say how vexed I feel to see vessels laden with potatoes, turnips, and other fresh provisions purchased at Venice and Trieste, lying for weeks together bound in these straits [Dardanelles] whilst their cargoes are rotting; all because the Admiral at Constantinople will neither keep a steamer here to assist wind-bound transport, or authorise me to hire a tug, *which the French* are constantly doing.

Yet, in spite of everything, by the end of March even the troops in the trenches were beginning to get their fair share. Mail and stores were reaching Balaclava from England within a fortnight, and each day the railway made positive progress. The authorities had no doubt that this was the key to one of their worst problems. They made sure that the construction gangs were properly treated, and they had no hesitation in tearing the town to pieces to hasten the work. George mentioned the subject in almost every letter for six or seven weeks.

4 February: The navvies have at last arrived, with all their railway and digging implements. Fine looking fellows they are; it makes one feel jolly to look at their faces, so well do they look compared with our half worn out, miserable, hungry looking, ill clad soldiers.

11 February: The main thoroughfare has been blocked up by the railway being made along it: all the traffic being now thrown into a very narrow, inconceivably muddy lane abounding in compound smells, which want of drainage, and the nasty habit of emptying slops etc. into the street produces. This road will shortly be turned into the main street; and houses, walls, etc., in front of them are to be pulled down to pave it. This is a proceeding which in England might seem strange, but in this part of the world it is a common, and the usual, method. Thus at the same time we pave, we widen the roads, but considerably diminish the number of houses – a loss which is rather a blessing than otherwise.

18 February: The railway is progressing in a most rapid style, and will before long I hope be engaged in carrying up stores and ammunition.

25 February: Our railway has made rapid progress. Already it has passed a little village called Kadikoi, outside this town about a mile and a half, and is close to the Cavalry camp. That portion of the line is now in use, and stores and wooden huts etc. are being carried up in large quantities by it: the large railway carts being dragged along the line by some gigantic English cart-horses. The railway, before it reaches the encampment before Sebastopol, will have to pass up a very steep hill, along the side of which are French entrenchments. Up this the trucks are to be pulled by rope by a stationary engine at the top. One great

good will at least be effected by the railroad. The men will not
have to be used as beasts of burden as they have been, and
even are up to the present time. Carts filled with warm clothing
etc. are dragged by men up to the front, much to the disgust
of the poor fellows who grumble much at being compelled to
do this kind of work.

1 March: Balaclava is improving very much in appearance, as
well as in sanitary condition. The streets are now getting well
macadamised, and so great is the change for the better, that
few who left here a few weeks since would now be able to
recognise it. The railway, I think, has done much in effecting this
improvement. It has now advanced to half way to Lord Raglan's,
and is used already extensively by the Commissariat.

11 March: The railway is progressing rapidly. The first accident
on it occurred last night by the overturning of a waggon, when
one man was killed, and another was obliged to have his leg
amputated.

22 March: To look at Balaclava and the neighbourhood, any
stranger would think that we are permanently settling here.
Huts are now built all over the place, and many regiments are
now using them as permanent barracks. The railway is rapidly
progressing and will soon be finished up to Headquarters. Now
warehouses have arrived and are to be placed near the quay,
and a complete set of warehousemen have come out with them.

Reid thought the navvies were pampered.

Soldiers were employed to make a wharf for them, soldiers
cleared away old houses to make room for sleeping huts for
them, and it was ordered that they were to live on board the
ships they came out in until their huts were ready. Cattle were
sent out to supply them with beef, and barrels of stout to quench
their thirst! Verily, the generals might have envied them, and
perhaps they did.

But George was more tolerant.

The navvies work well and willingly, reserving Sunday as a
day of rest, and one in which they may indulge a little in drink,

and consequently towards the afternoon or evening little groups
may be seen striving to get to their places of habitation in a
happy state of intoxication; but on other days you see little
of this.

Another comment came from an unexpected source.

We have at present staying in the town of Balaclava a
gentleman with his wife and family, whose name you are
probably by this time acquainted with. It is Mr Upton, the
son of Col. Upton, an English gentleman who from disagreeable
cause, I believe, left his native country, and settling in Russia
was employed by the Czar, and built the greater part of the
present fortifications of Sebastopol. This gentleman gave himself
up as a British subject when we came in front of Sebastopol,
and gave us much intelligence about the place. His statements,
I am told, were doubted as to their truthfulness, and he was
consequently detained here. He is a patient of mine, when
unwell, and I see much of him at times. He certainly seems to
me most anxious for the fall of Sebastopol, and has, I think,
been treated badly – as far as I can learn – in not having been
sent before to England. He has four of the prettiest little
children you have ever seen, who talk in English and tell all
their jokes and tales to their mother and servants in Russian.
It is pitiful to see such poor little creatures compelled to remain
in such a dirty place, without any means of amusement or
enjoyment.

Mr Upton says he is quite sure that the railway will be the
main instrument in the fall of Sebastopol. By its means we
shall be able to bring up to the front such quantities of ammunition etc., that we shall regularly blow the place to pieces about
them. I hope he may be right in his conjectures, and I believe
myself that until this railway is completed, you may not expect
to hear anything very decisive.

Medical arrangements were also undergoing a radical
change. New huts were daily increasing the accommodation
for cases at Balaclava General Hospital, and George

The railway at Balaclava

Castle Hospital, Balaclava

declared himself delighted with the standard of comfort and cleanliness now being achieved. Besides this, a new 'convalescent establishment' – in other words, a hutted hospital – was being constructed on the ridge below the old Genoese fort, overlooking the sea, where 'everything is carried on, on a most liberal scale, and the men are as comfortable and well provided for as they can be'. No less important was the arrival of female nurses, sent – at Lord Raglan's suggestion – somewhat unwillingly by Florence Nightingale, who had detached them from her rival, Mary Stanley.[6] When he first heard about Florence coming to Scutari, the previous autumn, George had taken up a condescending stance.

I see by the papers that Miss Nightingale is coming out with a number of nurses for the hospitals. Now nurses are very nice and useful people in Civil Hospitals, but I am afraid that with all Miss Nightingale's care and looking after her charges, she will not be able to put a stop to a number of little amours and intrigues which are sure to be carried on amongst a lot of comparatively healthy men, who have nothing but an injury, which in many cases may be slight, and which prevents their being in the Field.

But he soon altered his attitude, and was thankful for the party that reached Balaclava in late January.

Eight nurses have been sent up to the Hospital at Balaclava, fine matronly fat-looking women, with waists I will not say how large, in fact almost straight up and down, such as one looks at with pleasure in a London hospital. They will, I am sure, prove invaluable, and do more real good than 30 clumsy soldiers employed as hospital orderlies, who have no interest in the patients, save for the 4*d* a day which they receive in addition to their pay. I have tonight secured the services of one of these good women to attend upon a poor fellow, an Assistant-Surgeon who is very ill.

M

He repeated his praises in subsequent letters, and noted half-sadly:

One of our nurses is a Miss Stuart, sister of the Duchess of Somerset. The lady is, I am sure, perfectly mad. . . . She will persist in sitting up nearly every night with the worst fever cases, does her work also by day, and takes her rest by snatches of sleep, seldom removes her clothes, but when she is craved to take a little rest, wraps herself up in a cloak and lies down on the ground. She has already had an attack of erysipelas, and if she continues in her foolish ways, will probably get an attack of fever.

Gifts, useful and otherwise, flowed in for the sick.

It is very ridiculous to see the amount of rubbish anxious old ladies are daily sending out here for the 'poor sick soldiers', as they say. One old dame sent to the Hospital . . . two old pairs of boots, one old flannel dressing gown and an old night cap. Linen, also very old and useless, arrives here in quantities. A rag merchant might make a fortune from the surplus.

But a present of a ton of butter from Queen Victoria was gladly received.

It is most liberal and kind and will be much appreciated, as there is nothing more wished for by any of the men, particularly the sick, than this luxury; and it is far more sensible than the amount of rubbish and expensive things latterly sent out to 'the poor soldiers', as they are called: such as osmazone [*sic*], hare soup, preserved partridges, and the greatest absurdity of all, the enormous supply of old linen and in many cases old clothes, such as which could not possibly be worn by the men.

George's own medical duties included attendance upon the servants of officers and the multifarious employees of the Commissariat: Turks, Maltese, Spaniards, Italians, Russians, Frenchmen, Germans, Armenians, Poles, English and Irish. Many of the men were muleteers, and he regarded them as 'the worst specimens of their respective countries, or probably they would never have been here'.

I have now two huts at the General Hospital full of them. . . . The whole of my conversation with them is obliged to be carried out by means of an interpreter, but when I have to visit some of these unfortunate creatures (who are indeed a walking nest of parasites) without such aid, the only information I can obtain from them as regards their condition is 'Bono, Johnny' – a familiar, but at the same time not an intelligent answer to the signs I make to ascertain how they are.

For the Croat labourers, however, he expressed interest and almost affection.

A large number of Croatians are now in harbour, 750 in a small vessel capable of holding – according to military calculations – about 250. The men are rather mutinous in their behaviour, and have drawn their knives on several occasions and once against the Captain. They have come out, I am told, to work at the railway, and do in fact anything that is required of them. They are fine strong-looking fellows . . . packed between decks, little parcels of them playing cards, others wrapped up in their many-coloured garments smoking their long pipes with all the lazy indolence characteristic of their race.

Whatever the drawbacks of duty in Balaclava, George was well aware of his good luck and enjoyed his comforts to the full.

I am in right good health, living on the fat of the land, potted principally by Mr Gamble, of great repute out here. Shiploads of good things are continually arriving, and from them we are able to buy all we can desire; and although our servant is unable to make fine dishes, yet we can buy them already cooked and only to be warmed before eating. Sherry, very decent, can be had at about 3s a doz.

I am daily expecting the arrival of a goat which I have ordered to be purchased for me, for the purpose of supplying me with fresh milk every morning. I have not tasted milk since

I have been in the Crimea and intend soon thoroughly to enjoy this luxury.

What do you think of my extravagance? I saw a fine fat pig about to be killed on board one of the transports,[7] and in a luxurious mood I purchased one half of the animal for which I had to pay the small sum of £6–12s. I begin to feel ashamed at the price I have paid. It weighed 88 lbs. I shall charge it to our small mess account, and perhaps oblige some friends with a piece of it.

I have at last purchased a fine little pony for £13, which will I hope survive the summer. I have plenty of work for the little animal. I have also another servant – the old servant of Dr Pine who lately died here. He is a poor Pole, who was taken prisoner when we took possession of Balaclava; he is a most trustworthy man and a capital groom, and I consider myself fortunate in getting him, altho' our conversation is carried on by means of signs.

All he needed now, he wrote home in early March, was a pair of dark blue flannel trousers 'high in the waist', a small tent for summer use, and a pair of lace-up boots. Yet with every want satisfied, George was becoming restless. He was already sated with 'soft' living and bored with being a Staff doctor; and he began pulling strings, both in the Crimea and through friends at home.

I have written tonight to Dr Forrest, asking him to use his interest with the Director-General [Dr Andrew Smith] to getting me gazetted to the 3rd Battalion of the Rifle Brigade, which is now recruiting for foreign service in England. I hope I may be fortunate to get into this regiment, as I know the Colonel, as he has been staying with Dr Anderson here for the past 4 or 5 days, and has gone to England promoted to take command.

The Lawsons however were not enthusiastic, as they feared the Army might keep George for life.

I am sorry that you all seem to object to my getting into a regiment, but as I am now heartily tired of the Staff, having no regular servant, obliged so often to shift entirely for myself, and now compelled to pay £7 a month for my servants, I should be only too glad if I should find my name gazetted to a regiment. It will not prevent my leaving the service as soon as I feel inclined, that is to say when the war is over; and while I am in it I shall be infinitely more jolly, particularly as the warm weather is coming on, and I should like to see what is going on.

George had not long to wait. He never realised his gazette;[8] but the death of the Czar on 2nd March had put an end to all tentative negotiations for peace and strengthened the Russian will to resist. On their side the Allies were pouring in men and munitions, preparatory to a second massive bombardment of Sebastopol, due for the second week of April 1855.

15 : The last spring

To his cousin Mary: Thursday evening, 5th April

We have lately been in rather an anxious state about the commencement of the new attack on Sebastopol. Everything is now ready and it is reported that only some expected news from England is delaying the grand opening. It will be a much greater affair than the last time we began the siege, both being much more powerful, and more than double the amount of batteries to contend against.

Preparations are daily being made for the reception of the wounded in Balaclava, two hospital ships are now being fitted out, to remain stationary in the harbour, and a number of huts with beds all ready, are waiting the arrival of a number of unfortunates. I think that we shall do more than we did last time, indeed I do not think that there can be much doubt about it, as we have now so many appliances in our favour, which we did not then possess. ... The railway carries up enormous quantities of ammunition; and baggage horses, eighty in a string, may be seen daily toiling to the front under the weight of shot, shell and powder.

A large number of Sardinians[1] will soon arrive, 15,000 it is expected, as well as large reinforcements for the French. I think that with such an army as we shall soon have it will be no great credit if we do take Sebastopol, as it will have taken nearly all the European powers to reduce.

168

To his brother Ted : Sunday evening, 8th April

An order has come down tonight, in which it states that I am to have charge of one of the hospital huts. This I consider rather good, as I shall then have a large number of wounded under my own management, and shall give up my charge of sick and wounded Turks, Ilutians [*sic*], Spaniards, etc., all of whom I am getting rather tired of.

Great work is now going on in front of Sebastopol, fresh parallels[2] are being made, and we are getting much closer to the town. Working parties, 400 or 500 strong, are sent up from Balaclava to the front every day on mules, to do duty in the trenches, and are conveyed back again in some of the trucks.

An officer has just come in. He says that he has heard from official quarters that the cannonading commences again in earnest at day light tomorrow morning, or as the saying is here – 'the ball will open' at that hour . . . and so for the present I will wish you good night.

9 April: The firing commenced early this morning in good style. The Russians, I am told, were taken by surprise and did not return a single gun for ten minutes. Today has been without exception as wet and miserable as it could be, with a strong wind; notwithstanding this, I hear the guns still at work. The last news I have heard from the front is that we have silenced the G Battery, and that the Russian fire is more slack. Now we have commenced we are to continue night and day for a short time; and then, I suppose, we shall make the assault. If this is to be the case my hospital ship the *St. Hilda*[3] will soon be filled. We have, I think, accommodation in different hospitals for 2,000 wounded; I hope that we may not have need for more.

To his Mother : Sunday evening, 15th April

It is now almost a week since we opened fire with all our guns, at least it will be by day light tomorrow morning; and notwithstanding that the cannonading has not ceased, night or day, since that date, Sebastopol remains untaken. . . . Our fire still continues against the batteries and earthworks, which they have thrown up in such numbers and which are so difficult to destroy; the town consequently appears but little damaged.

. . . I was up at the front this afternoon, the place presents a wonderful and beautiful sight. From the whole length of our lines, and from all the works of the Russians there is a continuous line of smoke; one can hardly imagine so much ammunition being consumed and yet no decided effect produced. . . . Rumours are going about today that the storming is likely to take place early tomorrow morng. The truth of these reports is always doubtful, but that an assault will soon take place is believed by all, as if we cannot take Sebastopol by shot and shell, we must I suppose take it at the point of the bayonet; and secondly I do not think such large accommodation for wounded would have been prepared merely for bombardment. Our amount of casualties have not yet been large. . . . Scaling ladders, grappling irons and all the implements necessary for an assault have been sent to the front within the last day or two.

16 April: Everyone here is amazed at the little damage we are doing, and disgusted at seeing the termination of the siege almost as far off as ever. . . . My hospital ship, the *St Hilda*, has not yet a wounded man on board.

To his Father: Friday 20th April

Probably before this reaches you, you will have heard what a failure we have made with our siege train, that notwithstanding our cannonading Sebastopol still remains untaken, and that no assault has taken place, or is it indeed now expected. . . . It is said that Lord Raglan proposed to the French an assault, but they disapproved of such a proceeding, the town being far too strong, and besides *entre nous* I do not think the French can be relied upon in a case of assault as well as our men.

To his brother Fred: Monday 23rd April

I am sorry that I cannot give you any good account of our siege operations. Indeed I expect before this reaches you, indignant articles will have appeared in *The Times* and other papers, abusing the proceedings of the Commander-in-Chief. The feeling here is that he is a kind-hearted old woman, paying respect thus to his private and domestic qualities, but not saying much for him in his public capacity as head of a large army. I

cannot say how disgusted we all are at having made so little
impression on Sebastopol, many good men having been sacrificed
for nothing.

George's disappointment – as of all the Army – was
understandable; none the less, he was being less than fair
to Lord Raglan. The blunt facts were that, having now a
much larger and better equipped expeditionary force, the
French had consolidated their position as senior partner;[4]
that Canrobert, the French Commander-in-Chief, was being
worn down by repeated orders from Napoleon III – conveyed by Marshal Niel, his personal representative at HQ
– not to get committed: the reason being that the Emperor
had conceived a self-glorifying plan to come out to the
Crimea and lead his men to victory himself; finally, that
the British and French alike were thoroughly disheartened
by the apparent failure of the bombardment. Raglan did
not press for an assault; he was in no position to do so, but
in the eyes of his own people he had to bear the blame. His
troops were few and fed-up, and he had already lost the
majority of his seasoned campaigners. Moreover, as often
happens when morale falls, irritation and frustration boiled
over into a plethora of snide remarks about allies and
senior officers. The final fiasco occurred early in May, when
an allied sea-borne expedition against Kertch, on the Sea
of Azov, was literally recalled 'in midstream': thanks to
counter-orders from Paris, telegraphed by the new submarine cable recently laid between Varna and the Crimea.
This was the end for Canrobert who, timid and tired out,
was allowed to resign on 16th May. He was replaced by
Pélissier, a very different type of man.

But George Lawson was no longer on duty.

All during April he had been enjoying excellent health,
and – apart from the disappointment over the bombardment – generally in good spirits, retailing to his family all

kinds of news and gossip. He had heard all about the races
organised on the 7th by the 4th Division, and he commented
gratefully on the fresh green grass around the camps.

One hurdle race was for £300, and several heavy leaps had to
be taken, one in particular over a stone wall. All the races went
off very well with the exception of the steeplechase, when two
horses came down in attempting the stone wall. One officer of
the 34th was killed, and another of the Horse Artillery severely
injured. Wilkins of the 11th Hussars came in first with his horse,
having I am told gone over the ground most beautifully. He
seems to be very fortunate, winning nearly all the races he has
ridden himself.

On another day, much against his will, he had to attend
a flogging. On yet another he was able to say something
nice for once about the Turks.

We have lately received considerable reinforcements. Omar
Pascha has arrived from Eupatoria with 23,000 Turks, or rather,
I believe correctly speaking, Tunisians and Arabs. They are a
finer set of men than the miserable demoralised beings we have
so long been accustomed to look upon as Turks: well equipped
and in first rate order, with a large number of cavalry, and some
good horse artillery. Omar Pascha is himself a fine looking old
man, and from all his doings he must be a wonderfully clever
one.

He has just been furnished with a staff of English medical
officers, who have just arrived here, the Turkish surgeons to
act as their dressers, being but little else but barbers, resembling
the English doctors of olden time. They receive a pay from our
Government of 25s a day, the same pay as the civilian doctors,[5]
who have been sent out to assist the Medical Officers in the army.
Some of these civilians were fellow students with me at King's,
all my juniors, there are two at Smyrna Hospital and two with
the Turks. It is very disgusting to see these men, who I do not
certainly consider superior to me in their qualifications, receiving such a pay, when I as an unfortunate Staff Assistant-
Surgeon scarcely receive the amount which is given to the

navvies, and certainly not so much as any of the mechanics, viz. 7*s* 6*d* per day, exclusive of a few trifling extra allowances, which are not sufficient to pay for the horses or the servants you are compelled to keep.

In the week beginning 16th April he paid two visits to the Monastery of St George,[6] about six miles long the coast.

It is a wonderful looking place, built on the top of a cliff sloping down to the sea, with terraces and gardens in front, and extending to the edge of the water. The monastery . . . is rendered interesting from the excessive beauty of the spot, and from the number of old Russian priests being still allowed to remain there. There are also a number of Greek and Russian families still living there, and I saw without exception one of the prettiest Greek children, with some of the ugliest Russian.

Shortly afterwards:

I took a beautiful ride to Kamiesch Bay, about 9 miles from Balaclava. I was greatly and agreeably surprised with my visit. Kamiesch is to the French, what Balaclava is to the English. It is the harbour to which all the vessels for the French come in and discharge their cargo. Unlike Balaclava the neighbourhood all around is rather flat, the harbour is more than four times as large, and contains about five or six times as many vessels as Balaclava. There certainly is a degree of arrangement about the place which there is not about our little town. Everything has its place, huts are stored up in large numbers, and wood in sufficient quantities for six months' consumption, and commissariat provisions in large quantities. The shops consist, as they do in our case, of a number of wooden huts, with the frontage open and arranged in a somewhat tasteful manner. They are put up so as to form streets, all of which have a name, and from the presence of respectable looking women in the streets, the place assumes a degree of civilisation which is not witnessed in our Donnybrook Fair.

I am sorry to say that two or three cases of cholera[7] have appeared amongst our wounded. I hope we are not going to have another epidemic of this fearful malady. The weather is now very warm and beautiful, and we ought all to continue in good health.

Towards the end of April George's boredom with the lack of worthwhile patients was relieved by a visit from the British Ambassador to Turkey, Lord Stratford de Redcliffe, an imposing and important personage, much respected by the Turks, who had made full use of the freedom accorded to ambassadors before the days of the electric telegraph.

Lord Stratford with his lady and daughter arrived in Balaclava, a few days since, in the *Caradoc*. Lord Raglan with all his staff met them, and a guard of honour was waiting on the beach to receive them. They then proceeded to visit the different hospitals, and expressed great surprise at finding them all in such perfect order, expecting to see, I suppose, that disorder and bad arrangement which the papers would seem anxious to make out even now exists. My opinion is that no London Hospital was ever in better order than the hospitals here have been for the last 4 months.

May 1st came. George was comfortably housed, well fed, and plentifully supplied with letters and parcels from home. He received newspapers regularly and was particularly pleased with the copies of *Punch* and *The Illustrated London News*, which his father was forwarding to him. His immediate hope as always was for service with a regiment.[8]

As I have said before, my reason for wanting a regiment is that, on foreign service, it is always like home; and as I do not see the slightest chance of my getting home for a long time yet, I am of course anxious to settle myself as quietly and comfortably here as possible.

He did not know how soon his hopes were to be realised, though not in the way he had wanted or expected. Four days later he ended a letter to his father with:

I am sorry to say that I have been a little out of sorts the last 3 or 4 days, suffering I think from a little intermittent

fever, but as it has not been sufficient to incapacitate me from
work, you need not feel anxious about me.

The next thing his parents knew was a report from Dr
Anderson, dated 7th May. The Doctor wrote with heart-
warming affection, but barely concealed alarm.

Your son George has got an attack of fever which, though at
present slight, prevents his writing to you. I need not say that
he is well looked after, as I love him as I would a young brother,
and I have him in a cool room in my house with a first rate
London nurse[9] to look after him, who knew him at the University in London. Nothing shall be wanting to bring him round
again, and I trust in God that he may soon be able to speak for
himself. . . . Miss Nightingale, who has come up here on a
visit, has just called to see him, and has taken a great interest
in him. She says the nurse is one of the best she has.

According to medical opinion, George's illness – in all
probability – was typhus, contracted from attending muleteers and conveyed by a body louse. It was not cholera,
and in view of the previous attack of fever (at Varna in
August 1854) was not likely to have been typhoid.[10]
The reference to Florence Nightingale is of great interest:
in general, because this was her first visit to the Crimea;
and in particular because within a few days she too collapsed with 'Crimean fever', which in her case may have
been either typhoid or typhus. She was attended by Dr
Anderson, who was also looking after George, and who told
the Lawsons that 'poor Miss Nightingale is laid up with a
similar attack'. The condition of the two patients gave
cause for anxiety for about a fortnight[11] – in the case of
Florence, of course, there was national consternation – in
the case of George, a touching letter from his father to
Dr Anderson, dated 21st May, communicated the deep
family distress.

I know not how sufficiently to thank you for your very kind

letter of the 7th inst., and although I feel most grateful to the
Almighty to hear from you that my dear son George is surrounded by such warm-hearted good friends as yourself and
others, I confess to you that I feel more than I can express, in
reading what I am sure you have written, a faithful account of
the malady from which he is now suffering. He is indeed my
dear Sir, in every sense of the word a most excellent young
man, he has always proved himself a most exemplary dutiful
son, a kind and affectionate brother, and a sincerely attached
friend to any who have had the pleasure of becoming acquainted
with him. This is saying a great deal, but although said by his
Father, I can assure you that he deserves all and more that I
can say of him.

Under any circumstances these recollections are very con-
soling that above all your kind expressions of his worth, your
hitherto repeated acts of what I may truly say devoted kindness
to him, and your promise that all shall be done for him that
human aid can procure, it is indeed very gratifying to the
feelings of myself, his Mother, and the rest of the family, to
receive these kind assurances from you, and lays us under a
debt of gratitude that I fear we can never discharge. I will
however venture to say that I will do my best when opportunity
offers and in the interim, I must as in the case of my much
beloved son trust in the goodness of God.

On 11th May Dr Hall visited George,[12] and on the 18th
Dr Anderson was able to tell the Lawsons that he was
over the worst.

The day after I wrote you he became senseless after fainting
several times, and it was only by *pouring* brandy down his
throat and giving him injections of strong essence of beef that,
under God, we were able to preserve his vitality. He is now quite
sensible, free from fever, but desperately weak.

Two days later George wrote himself.

I have, I believe, had a very severe attack of fever, and am
now suffering from the results, and the treatment. I am, as you

will see by this writing, very weak, but what troubles me most is a terrible sore state of the back of the neck from continued blistering; as far as regards appearance, I do not think I am much altered.

His recovery was slow. The blisters gave him a great deal of pain, and his initial convalescence was prolonged. Meanwhile, his name had appeared in General Orders for permission to return to England on sick leave. On 1st June Dr Anderson wrote to say that, as his own health had 'broken up', he would be bringing George back home himself in a party of wounded and invalids aboard the *Saldanha*[13] sailing transport, due to leave Balaclava about 9th or 10th June.

On 8th June George wrote his last letter from the Crimea. His neck, though still sore, was at last healing.

I think I ought to think myself rather a fortunate fellow in being alive, to tell the tale of having had two attacks, and very severe ones of fever, when so many have died in their first, and very few can say that they have had a second; however if I reach home safely this time, I do not think I shall stand much chance of having a third.

His interest in the war had revived. The second expedition to Kertch at the end of May had proved a complete success, and on 6th June the bombardment of Sebastopol was renewed, preceding the capture of two important positions: the Mamelon by the French, the Quarries by the British. Everything was now ready for the final offensive, timed for 18th June, the fortieth anniversary of the Battle of Waterloo, the memory of which would be buried in a glorious victory by the two former antagonists. The objective of the French was the Malakoff, of the British the Redan: these were the two main defence works of Sebastopol, and once in allied hands the town would fall. But both assaults failed with heavy loss; and the depression of the defeat was deepened by the ravages of cholera, which carried off Lord Raglan on 28th June.

George was no longer in Balaclava to hear the sad news. On 23rd June the *Saldanha* put in at Malta, and on 18th July a letter posted at Gibraltar revealed that he had had a relapse, this time from polyneuritis, a recognised complication of typhus.

I am still in a very feeble condition, and you will, I am sure, be sorry to hear I have entirely lost the use of my legs, and in some degree that of my hands also, but as my bodily health is so good and my appetite rather voracious, I think that as I gain strength I shall recover the use of my limbs again.

The *Saldanha* docked at Portsmouth in the first fortnight of August. After nearly seventeen months Dr George Lawson was home again.

Epilogue

Less than a month after George's return to England, on 8th September 1855, the French succeeded in capturing the Malakoff, but the British failed at the Redan. On the following day the Russians blew up the harbour installations and evacuated the south side of Sebastopol. The war did not end at once, however. The allies spent a comparatively comfortable and carefree winter in the ruins of the town before peace was signed in Paris in March 1856. For the British and French 'the unnecessary war' had lasted almost exactly two years.

After an illness of five months, George recovered; but it was not a total recovery, and he suffered for the rest of his life from a weak heart and an impaired circulation.[1] However, a year after his return in August 1856, Elizabeth Woodward was able to write this letter from St John's House to Florence Nightingale, lately arrived from the Crimea:

Madam,

I beg leave to express the pleasure I feel at hearing of your safe arrival in England and your native home, and at the same time to say how deeply I feel your kindness in allowing me to attend Mr Lawson on his voyage when he was invalided at Balaclava. Often I nursed him in fever then as he became perfectly paralysed in a few days after he came on board the *Saldanha*,[2] and continued to grow weaker during a tedious voyage of eight weeks and four days – all that time for one hour either night or day I never left him. I know Madam how highly gratifying it will be to you to hear that Mr Bowman and Dr Todd[3] did not hesitate to say that, owing to my exertions,

Mr Lawson's life was preserved until he reached England, when
the Lord blest the means these gentlemen took for his recovering. He is now quite well and commenced his profession at
63 Park Street, Grosvenor Square, and I know he only waits
an opportunity of acknowledging your kindness.

I beg to remain, Madam

Your much obliged and humble servant

Elizabeth Woodward

There remains a balance of 3 pounds 2 shillings as Mr Bracebridge[4] only paid me for four weeks on the journey which lasted
as long as I stated in the first [part] of my letter.

As to the end of the tale – despite a weakened constitution George Lawson enjoyed a long and successful career,
dying in 1903 at the age of seventy-one. He practised both
as a general and an ophthalmic surgeon, was connected for
many years with two hospitals – Moorfields and the Middlesex – and built up a private practice in Harley Street as
well. He was the author of several authoritative works on
eye medicine and surgery, and was accorded deserved
honours, including membership of the Council of the Royal
College of Surgeons and the post of Surgeon Oculist to
Queen Victoria.

The Crimea left its mark upon his mind too. He never
forgot his experiences on the Heights, he never forgot the
Army and the soldiers who suffered, and he would often
take extraordinary trouble to help those who were injured
or disabled to obtain a proper pension or compensation.
Indeed, his knowledge of suffering informed all his actions.

He did not stop in his treatment at simply prescribing drugs
or lotions. He would instruct a mother how to feed, to clothe,
and to train her child, often entering into much detail as to the
preparation of the food. He would tell a patient in whom nothing could be done to restore sight what he could still do and
how to get work to earn a livelihood. Many of those who see
out-patients have doubtless wished that they could prescribe

for some of them food instead of medicine. Mr Lawson actually did this, having an arrangement with a neighbouring butcher by which he could order patients so many pounds of meat. Nor did Mr Lawson's generosity to out-patients end with supplying sound advice and meat; many a patient to whom some more than usually disastrous circumstance had occurred would be led quietly aside and return with a smiling face a and closed palm.[5]

As a general surgeon he was both courageous and pains-taking; fearless in undertaking any operation, however formid-able, if in his sound and sagacious judgment he had satisfied himself of its wisdom and justification. . . . To his house-surgeons, dressers, and clinical assistants, he was ever an adorable chief. . . . Though conservative by instinct, he was a reformer in matters of hospital construction and in his scrupulous regard for cleanly surgery. To his instrumentality the Middlesex Hospital was indebted for the introduction of teak wood flooring, and his example in his own wards was rapidly followed by others. He, too, was one of the first to discard the time-honoured frock coat, soiled with the blood stains of a hundred operations, in favour of a washable overall, though at first his zeal in this innov-ation was the subject of not a little banter.[6]

George Lawson became the father of seven sons. The daughter of one of them inherited his Crimean letters – which is the reason for this book.

Notes

CHAPTER 1

1. Information about the Lawsons is derived from family sources, with additional notes about the wine business from *Harper's Manual*, 1915.

2. Information and quotations concerning Forest Hill are mainly taken from *One Hundred Years, the Story of Christ Church, Forest Hill*, by the Rev. R. P. Wernham, MBE, AKC. Thanet Press, Margate, 1954.

3. William Cobbett, 1762–1835: agriculturalist, politician and journalist.

4. Information about George Lawson's medical training and his instructors at King's College is provided by (*a*) *The Lancet* 1847, Vol. 2, p. 357, (*b*) *King's and Some King's Men*, by H. Willoughby Lyle, MD, FRCS. OUP, 1935/1950. (*c*) Dr F. F. Cartwright, LRCP, MRCS, FFARCS.

5. Quotation from the records of St John's House, now at St Thomas's Hospital, by courtesy of the archivist. The Bishop of London's formula at the foundation meeting on 18th July 1848 ran: 'An Institution of Sisters, but there would be no vows, no poverty, no monastic obedience, no celibacy, no engagements, no cloistered seclusion, no tyranny exercised over the will or conscience; but a full, free and willing devotion to the cause of Christian charity.'

CHAPTER 2

1. The medical history incorporated in this chapter is derived from study of the appropriate works listed under Sources; but particularly from help generously given by Mr J. K. Crellin of Wellcome Historical Medical Museum and Library, and by Dr F. F. Cartwright of King's College Hospital.

2. Information about King's College Hospital mainly derives from the book by H. Willoughby Lyle, and from Dr Cartwright.

183

3. *The First Anaesthetic: the Story of Crawford Long*, by Frank Kells Boland, MD. University of Georgia Press, Athens, 1950, pp. 19–20.

4. *Regulations for the Management of Army Hospitals*. War Office, 1845.

5. *A History of Medicine*, by Douglas Guthrie, MD, FRCS. ED, FRSE. Nelson, 1958, p. 301.

6. Quoted from Dr John Hall's *Medical Memorandum*, Hall Papers, Millbank. It is reprinted in full on pp. 302–3 in Professor Percival Kirby's recent biography of Dr Andrew Smith, Head of the Army Medical Department during the Crimean War, entitled *Sir Andrew Smith. His Life, Letters and Works*. Balkema, Cape Town/Amsterdam, 1965. It was also quoted in *The Illustrated London News* of 23rd September 1854, and has been referred to in many books about the Crimea, often out of context. In fact anaesthetics were commonly used during the campaign.

7. Information and advice from Mr and Mrs Philip Proffitt, Dulverton, Somerset.

CHAPTER 3

1. The whole of this paragraph derives from a lecture entitled *Teeth and Tail in the Crimea*, given by Major-General R. E. Barnsley, CB, MC, MA, MB, B.CH, at the Osler Club on 7th June 1962, and published in *Medical History*, 1963, Vol. 7.

2. Military medical history up to the middle of the nineteenth century, as outlined in this section of the book derives from (*a*) *Roll of Commissioned Officers in the Medical Service of the British Army 1727–1898*, by Charles William Johnston, CB, MA, MD. Aberdeen, at the University Press, 1917. (*b*) *Mars and Aesculapius*, an address given at the Royal Army Medical College on 3rd December 1963 by Major-General R. E. Barnsley. (*c*) Various histories listed under Sources. (*d*) Conversations with Lieut-General Sir Neil Cantlie, KBE, CB, MC, FRCS, KHS, former Director-General of the Army Medical Services and historian of the Royal Army Medical Corps.

3. These were the principal activities of Florence Nightingale's nurses when they first arrived at Scutari.

4. All information about Dr Andrew Smith, including the quotations, in this chapter is taken from Professor Percival R. Kirby's biography.

5. Kirby, p. 282.

6. Kirby, p. 291.

7. The duties of the members of the Hospital Conveyance Corps
were to carry the wounded quickly from the battlefield, to supply
hospitals with NCOs and orderlies, to take care of the ambulance
carts and horses, and to furnish servants for the officers of the
General Medical Staff. See *A Treatise on the Transport of Sick
and Wounded Troops*, by Deputy Inspector-General T. Longmore,
CB. HMSO, 1869.

8. Kirby, p. 285.

CHAPTER 4

1. See Kirby, pp. 273–4.
2. Cattell Papers, Millbank.
3. *Memories of the Crimean War, January 1855 to June 1856*, by
Douglas Arthur Reid, MD. St Catherine's Press, London, 1911,
pp. ix–x.
4. Information kindly supplied by the National Maritime Museum,
Greenwich.
5. The presence of French detachments inspired the following
message from the Special Correspondent of *The Times*, published
on 4th April 1854: '. . . The most perfect good feeling pervades
the allies. The most sensitive of Frenchmen could see nothing in
our covered ensigns to revive the least bit of bitterness or
international hatred. It was pleasant to witness the meeting of
two armies which have never yet had a friendly rencontre. On
the soil of Malta French and English troops have stood for the
first time without preparing for the shock of battle, and the
cheers which are now ringing from shore to sea till the rocks
re-echo, are no longer ominous of conflict.'
6. *British Malta*, Vol. 1, 1800–72, by A. V. Laferla. Malta Government Printing Office, 1938, p. 223. The author also records:
'Even at the present day, a spendthrift is often asked, "Do you
think that this is the time of the Crimea?" '
7. *Malta*, by Sir Harry Luke, KCMG, Lieutenant-Governor of Malta,
1930–8. Harrap, 1949, p. 6. Historical information about Malta
is taken from both Laferla and Luke.
8. From *The Times* of 11th March 1854: 'The *Kangaroo* is a splendid
new Clyde-built screw steamer 1,874 tons . . . and fitted with
oscillating geared engines of 300 horse power. She belongs to the
Australian Pacific Line, in connexion with the West India mail
steamers, being intended to run between Panama and Sydney.
Her arrangements for the transport of troops are on the liberal

and commodious side. The chief saloon, which is beautifully
fitted, and supplied with abundance of light and ventilation, is
allotted to the commissioned officers. . . . The *Kangaroo* has a
flush deck, the staterooms reserved for officers being amidships.
The open spaces and corridors between the berths forward and
the after part of the ship are slung with hammocks for the men.'

CHAPTER 5

1. Letter to *The Times* of 2nd May 1854.

2. On 19th June George Lawson wrote to his father: 'I have told
   you in some of my other letters that we are very much annoyed
   with dogs, which abound in great numbers both in the town and
   in the country. They are a mongrel set of creatures and when met
   singly will run away, almost at the sight of a man, but unfortunately when in numbers they have more courage, and will
   attack you even when on horseback. The other day, when some
   distance in the country, I was attacked by two of these great
   beasts, more resembling wolves than anything else you can
   imagine. I put my horse to his fullest speed and although pursued
   by them for some distance, they soon got tired and let me go
   away. . . .'

3. The Crystal Palace, built in Hyde Park for the Great Exhibition
   of 1851, was transferred to Sydenham and reopened in 1854.

CHAPTER 6

1. Cattell Papers, Millbank.

2. In a letter dated 28th July to his sister Ellen (Nelly), George
   described the difficulties of driving bullock waggons up the steep
   hill to the new camp-site, and added: 'We are now encamped on
   the opposite side of the bay to where we were first, as close as
   we are able to be to the sea, at the top of a high cliff, something
   like the Shakespeare cliff at Dover, commanding a magnificent
   view of the country on the opposite side with all the French
   encampments and also of the sea and harbour, so that we are
   able to see every vessel coming in or out of Varna, and look
   enviously on those vessels which we suppose are carrying the
   mails to England, and wish ourselves inside the envelopes instead
   of the letters.'

3. Dr Dumbreck's report is quoted from p. 9 of Vol. 2 of the official
   medical history of the Crimean campaign compiled by Dr

Andrew Smith, and entitled *The Medical and Surgical History of the British Army, which served in Turkey and the Crimea during the War against Russia in the years 1854–5–6*. London, 1858.

4. Kirby, p. 286.

5. Quotation from *Biography and the 'Amateur' Historian*, by W. H. Greenleaf, contributed to *Victorian Studies*, December 1959.

6. All the quotations from Dr Hall are taken from his diaries and other papers, deposited at Millbank, except where stated: e.g. from Mitra's biography of Hall or Kirby's biography of Dr Andrew Smith. See Sources.

7. Country carts.

8. George described the fleet as 'consisting of 100 English transports (some of the finest Liverpool vessels) and towed by 50 steam vessels, each of course also filled with troops. Each steamer towed two vessels. There were also about 50 vessels belonging to the Turks, and I should think about 150 belonging to the French, so that there was a fleet of about 350 or 400 strong. The English sailed in lines parallel to one another, and in that order we anchored when we arrived off here [Calamita Bay]. The French were in miserable little vessels, transports hired from all parts. We were accompanied by a large number of Men-of-War in line of battle, and Men-of-War steamers, both English and French.'

CHAPTER 7

1. A portion of this letter is quoted on p. 1.

2. Much of the inefficiency and lack of preparation on the part of the British Army, as revealed in the Crimean campaign, must be attributed to the rigid control exercised by the Duke over military affairs in the thirty-five years after Waterloo.

3. *The Medical and Surgical History etc.*, Vol. II, p. 253.

4. Hall Papers, Millbank.

5. As Note 3, pp. 253–4.

6. *Report upon the State of the Hospitals of the British Army in the Crimea and Scutari*. London, 1855, p. 177.

7. See Note 4 to Chapter 13.

8. As Note 6, pp. 194–5.

CHAPTER 8

1. A remark attributed to General Sir George Cathcart, commander of the 4th Division.

2. HMS *Tiger* ran aground and was captured off Odessa in May 1854.

3. *Letters from the Black Sea, during the Crimean War 1854–5*, by Admiral Sir Leopold George Heath, KCB. Richard Bentley and Son, 1897, pp. 79–80.

4. Hall Papers, Millbank.

5. Probably the family nurse.

CHAPTER 9

1. The French Minié rifle was the first weapon to discharge cylindrical-conoidal bullets. Muzzle-loading, length of barrel 39 inches, weight 10 lb 8·75 oz, sighted up to 1,000 yards. Adopted by the British Army in 1851.

2. Letter dated 7th November 1854.

CHAPTER 10

1. Dr Spence was one of the three Hospital Commissioners. See p. 132.

CHAPTER 11

1. Hall Papers, Millbank; and as Note 2, p. 27.

2. *The Medical and Surgical History etc.*, Vol. II, pp. 27–8.

3. See *The Chemist and the Crimea*, by Lt-Col M. E. S. Laws, OBE, MC, FR. HIST. S, in *The Pharmaceutical Journal* of 5th February 1955 for further information.

4. Successor to Dr Forrest as PMO of the 3rd Division.

5. All statistics and contingent information are taken from *The Medical and Surgical History etc.*, Vol. II, pp. 202 *et seq.*

6. *Ibid*, p. 182.

7. *Ibid*, p. 209.

8. This total was subsequently corrected to 3,085.

CHAPTER 12

1. This small port had been held by allied troops since the initial landing in the Crimea in September 1854. Herds of cattle and sheep were maintained in the immediate area and shipped regularly by sea to Balaclava. The Russians, however, had reoccupied all the country between Eupatoria and Sebastopol.

2. Letter to *The Times* of 8th November 1854.

3. See Note 3 to Chapter 8. Heath, p. 169.

4. Letter to *The Times* of 25th November 1854.

5. Heath, pp. 178–9.

6. Heath, pp. 180–1.

7. W. H. Russell's letter to *The Times* of 1st December 1854.

8. W. H. Russell's letter to *The Times* of 13th January 1855.

9. *Report of the Commission of Inquiry into the Supplies of the British Army in the Crimea.* London, 1855–6, p. 1.

10. Quoted from the letter by Commissary-General Filder dated 27th February 1856, annexed to the above Report.

11. Heath criticised Mr Filder for 'want of foresight, and bad calculation as to the number of horses required; to which may be added a total want of even an attempt at taking care of the animals he did provide. . . . When the poor beasts had travelled six or seven miles, heavily laden, on wretched roads, and returned the same distance, they were turned out in an open yard, eighteen inches deep in mud, off which mud they ate their barley and chopped straw. There were no stable keepers separate from the drivers, and the latter, being as tired after their day's work as the beasts themselves, acted upon a principle which a campaigning life tends to foster, that of looking after No. 1 first.' Heath, p. 167.

12. *Supplies Commission Report, etc.*, p. 9.

13. *Ibid*, p. 13.

14. Duties shared with the Ordnance Department.

15. Letter to *The Times* of 2nd January 1855.

16. *The Royal Army Service Corps*, by John Fortescue. CUP, 1930, p. 157.

CHAPTER 13

1. All the information concerning the work of the Hospitals Commission is taken from the *Report upon the State of the Hospitals of the British Army in the Crimea and Scutari*. London,

1855. It was Dr Andrew Smith, Director-General of the Army
Medical Department, who first suggested the appointment of
such a Commission.

2. *Hospitals Commission Report*, p. 14.

3. See p. 143.

4. Dr Hall noted: 'The *Andes* and *Cambria* were told off by Admiral
Boxer as Hospital Ships and were equipped at Varna for that
purpose in August 1854. But they were filled and overcrowded
with Troops by the Authorities and were never employed as
Hospital Ships at all. They were ill calculated for the service
they were intended for, and the Captain of the *Andes* was a
drunken ill-conditioned man and subsequently occasioned much
embarrassment by trans-shipping the stores to another vessel –
without giving notice or anyone knowing where they [were].
In December they were accidentally discovered in the store of
the Light Division, the packages all broken open and the things
plundered.' Hall Papers, Millbank.

5. *Hospitals Commission Report*, p. 16.

6. *Ibid*, pp. 18–19.

7. *Ibid*, p. 16.

8. Heath, p. 179.

9. Hall Papers, Millbank.

10. See *The Life and Letters of Sir John Hall*, by S. M. Mitra.
Longmans, 1911, pp. 352–3. It is of interest that the scarcity of
medical orderlies was due to the scale laid down by the Adjutant-
General's Order of 18th October 1854, viz. four orderlies per 100
invalids embarked.

11. As the Press made much of the Lawson *affaire*, George's father
felt constrained eventually to write to *The Times* on 10th
February 1855 – by which time George had himself been transferred to Balaclava on duty – as follows:

'Sir – Will you allow me through your widely-circulated
journal to contradict a report that Dr Lawson, who has incurred
the censure of Lord Raglan, is a member of my family? The
name of my son is George, late of King's College Hospital, and
he has been serving as staff assistant-surgeon at the camp before
Sebastopol from the first commencement of the siege, and he has
only been stationed at Balaclava since the 17th ult., when he
was sent there on duty.

I am, Sir, your obedient servant
William Lawson.

39 St Mary-at-Hill, London
and Forest Hill, Sydenham.'

12. Dr Pine had succeeded Dr Forrest as PMO of the 3rd Division at the end of December 1854. Dr Forrest was first posted to Scutari, then invalided home.

13. Major-General Sir Richard England, commander of the 3rd Division.

14. Longmans, 1961.

15. *Supplies Commission Report, etc*, p. 39.

16. *Report to the Rt. Hon. Lord Panmure of the Proceedings of the Sanitary Commission Dispatched to the Seat of War in the East 1855–56.* London, 1857. Preamble.

17. On 8th March 1855, somewhat belatedly, Dr Hall set up his own Board of Health in the Crimea to investigate sanitary matters. But the Commissions were already upon him.

18. *Notes on Matters affecting the Health, Efficiency, and Hospital Administration of the British Army*, by Florence Nightingale. London, 1858, p. xxxvi.

19. *Ibid*, pp. 242–3.

20. *Report of the Commissioners appointed to inquire into the Regulations affecting the Sanitary Condition of the Army, the Organization of Military Hospitals, and the Treatment of the Sick and Wounded.* London, 1858.

21. *First, Second and Third Report from the Select Committee on the Army before Sebastopol.* London, 1855.

22. See Kirby, pp. 314–21.

23. All the correspondence throughout the campaign was subsequently published in two volumes under the title of *Précis, or Descriptive Index of all Letters bearing on Matters relating to the Army, etc.* London, 1858. As noted, Smith was also responsible for the publication in two volumes of the official medical history of the campaign, *The Medical and Surgical History of the British Army which served in Turkey and the Crimea, etc.* London, 1858.

24. *Report from the Select Committee on the Medical Department (Army), together with the Proceedings of the Committee, Minutes of Evidence, etc.* London, 1856.

25. For a short but highly readable account of these developments see *Not Least in the Crusade. A Short History of the Royal Army Medical Corps*, by Peter Lovegrove. Gale and Polden, 1951, pp. 11–19.

CHAPTER 14

1. Dr Arthur Anderson, Principal Medical Officer, Balaclava.

2. The information and quotations concerning Dr Reid are all taken from *Memories of the Crimean War: January 1855 to June 1856*, by Douglas Arthur Reid, MD. St Catherine's Press, London, 1911. Preface and Chapters I–IV. See also pp. 30–1.

3. Not of course, Dr Arthur Anderson, PMO at Balaclava.

4. Reid added: 'The Authorities, in recognition of her benevolent services, awarded her the Crimean Medal. Some years afterwards I met her at Charing Cross. The medal first attracted my eye, and on looking up I recognised her dusky countenance. Of course I stopped her, and we had a short talk together about Crimean times. She had a store at Kadikoi, near Balaclava, for some time, where she sold all sorts of commodities, clothing and articles of food that were luxuries to us. I need not say that she was largely patronised. Her store appears as a landmark in one of the maps in Russell's book on the war. It is there called "Mrs Seacole's Hut".'

   Mrs Seacole was in fact one of the many sutlers or camp followers who sold goods (mostly food and drink) to the troops, and who followed the Army on every campaign, appearing in the most unlikely places. They were present in great numbers in Balaclava and Kadikoi.

5. See p. 48.

6. See *Florence Nightingale*, by Cecil Woodham-Smith. Constable, 1950, p. 192.

7. Reid commented: 'The transports in the harbour were our shops. The captains and pursers were good enough to spare us many comforts, such as fresh bread, a fowl, turkey, sometimes a joint of fresh meat, a goose, sugar, butter, and pickles. Also various drinkables – beer, wine, spirits, in fact anything they could spare out of their stores. With these we loaded the hospital panniers – we never returned to camp empty-handed.'

8. In fact, he was gazetted to the Rifle Brigade on 1st May 1855, but, falling ill about the same day, a bout of typhus put an end to all further service. See Chapter 15. He resigned his commission in 1856.

CHAPTER 15

1. The dispatch of Sardinian troops was a political gesture by Cavour, who was hoping (and his hopes were realised in 1859)

that, in return, Napoleon III would help him drive the Austrians out of Lombardy. The Sardinians acquitted themselves with distinction in the Crimea, and assisted the French defeat the Russians at the Battle of the Tchernaya on 16th August 1855.

2. Trenches dug parallel to the face of the works being attacked.

3. It is presumed from this reference that George was attached to the *St Hilda*, either in place of superintending a hospital hut or in addition to that duty.

4. The French had about 90,000 men, the British 30,000. Moreover, the French and Sardinians together had relieved the British of the right of the line.

5. For an expert account of the scheme for recruiting civilian doctors for the Crimea, of the civil hospitals at Smyrna and Renkioi, together with a reference to the pre-fabricated hospital huts designed by Isambard Kingdom Brunel, the railway engineer, see 'The Civil Hospitals in the Crimea, 1855–1856', by John Shepherd, FRCS.ED, published in the *Proceedings of the Royal Society of Medicine*, March 1966, Vol. 59, No. 3, pp. 199–204.

6. The Monastery was also the terminus of the submarine cable from Varna. George wrote on 30th April 1855: 'The Electric Telegraph across the Black Sea has now been completed. It extends from St George's Monastery on the shore, to some place near Varna. From there it is carried to Bucharest, where it becomes continuous with the line from Vienna. News will therefore be forwarded to England in a very short space of time, and you will be able to hear in the evening what we have been doing in the Crimea in the morning. The space of time to transmit a message will, I think, be 6 or 7 hours owing to the number of places where there are breakages, and the message has then to be transmitted again from the one to the other. Thus a portion of the time is taken up, which cannot be avoided, as for some reason it is impossible to have a continuous wire. I saw the Telegraph working the other day, when I was at the Monastery.'

7. This was the beginning of the second epidemic of cholera, when 1,400 men died between May and August 1855. See Chapter 11.

8. See note 8 to Chapter 14.

9. Elizabeth Woodward, a St John's House nurse. See p. 5. All the doctors spoke well of her, and she accompanied George back to England. George wrote on 24th May: 'I do not think I have mentioned to you that, during the whole of my illness, I have been well looked after by a capital nurse, sent to me by Miss Nightingale, who arrived at Balaclava soon after I was taken ill. Strange to say, it is the same woman who attended Mrs Bowman

in her last serious illness after her confinement. She certainly has done her duty towards me.'

10. I am indebted to Dr Kenneth D. Keele, MD, FRCP, for the following notes on George's two illnesses:

First illness: The main features of this illness consist of fever, delirium, headache, of some ten days duration, with 'profuse haemorrhage from the bowels'. It is clear that the haemorrhage was severe and threatened life. The whole clinical picture fits in with a diagnosis of typhoid fever. Ulceration of the ileum [Peyer's patches] is a feature of typhoid which produces brisk large haemorrhages late in the disease. These are a common cause of death.

Second Illness: If the first illness was typhoid, it is unlikely that the second one would be the same since the patient would be immune. This illness has an insidious onset with fever and minor symptoms. At the end of a week Dr Anderson is worried about him. By the tenth day he is delirious. After three weeks he is still extremely weak and tremulous. His main symptoms later are due to the blisters on the back of the neck, probably used to relieve headache or delirium. There is no mention of any bowel symptoms in this attack. The clinical picture, scanty as it is, suggests typhus.

11. When both patients were over the worst, they were taken up to the Castle Hospital for convalescence.

12. From a letter dated 11th May 1855 from Dr Anderson to George's father: 'Dr Hall came to see him today, he takes a great interest in him (as indeed does everyone who knows him), and he agreed with me that there was no cause for alarm at present, and told your son to get well and get home as soon as possible.'

13. Dr Hall made the following note about the *Saldanha:* 'This vessel was fitted out in England complete in every respect for the conveyance of invalids from the Crimea to England.' Hall Papers, Millbank.

EPILOGUE

1. The following passage occurs in the Obituary Notice published in *The Lancet* on 24th October 1903: 'His pulse-rate was always remarkably slow and his hands were cold and livid. Those who have followed him round the hospital will recall the frequent pauses that he made in ascending any stairs, pauses always enlivened by charming conversation on the wide and diverse subjects in which he was interested.'

2. The *Saldanha*, it will be remembered, was a *sailing* transport, and in his last letter home, dated 18th July 1855, George wrote: 'We succeeded yesterday in getting halfway thro' the straits [of Gibraltar], but a head wind unfortunately drove us a long way back again.'

3. Two of his instructors at King's. See pp. 4–5.

4. Mr Bracebridge looked after Florence Nightingale's financial affairs in the Crimea.

5. From *The Lancet* of 24th October 1903.

6. From *The British Medical Journal* of 17th October 1903.

Sources – a select list

UNPUBLISHED

The Memoirs of William Cattell.
The Papers of Sir John Hall.
The Letters of George Lawson.
The Records of St John's House.

NEWSPAPERS, PERIODICALS AND PAMPHLETS

The British Medical Journal.
Harper's Manual.
The Illustrated London News.
The Lancet.
Mars and Aesculapius.
Medical History.
The Pharmaceutical Journal.
The Proceedings of the Royal Society of Medicine.
Regulations for the Management of Army Hospitals.
Teeth and Tail in the Crimea.
The Times.
A Treatise on the Transport of Sick and Wounded Troops.
Victorian Studies.

OFFICIAL REPORTS

Report upon the State of the Hospitals of the British Army in the Crimea and Scutari. 1855.

First, Second and Third Report from the Select Committee on the Army before Sebastopol, 1855.

Report of the Commission of Inquiry into the Supplies of the British Army in the Crimea. 1855–6.

Report from the Select Committee on the Medical Department
(Army), together with the Proceedings of the Committee,
Minutes of Evidence, etc. 1856.

Report to the Rt Hon Lord Panmure of the Proceedings of the
Sanitary Commission dispatched to the Seat of War in the
East, 1855–6. 1857.

Report of the Commissioners appointed to inquire into the Regulations affecting the Sanitary Condition of the Army, etc. 1858.

Précis, or Descriptive Index of all Letters bearing on Matters relating
to the Army, etc. Two volumes. 1858.

The Medical and Surgical History of the British Army which served
in Turkey and the Crimea, etc. Two volumes. 1858.

BOOKS

BIOGRAPHY

The Life and Letters of Sir John Hall, by S. M. Mitra. Longmans,
1911.

The Life of Florence Nightingale, by E. T. Cook. Two volumes.
Macmillan, 1913.

Florence Nightingale, by Cecil Woodham-Smith. Constable, 1950.

In a Liberal Tradition, by Victor Bonham-Carter. Constable, 1960.

Sir Andrew Smith. His Life, Letters and Works, by Percival R. Kirby.
Balkema, Cape Town/Amsterdam, 1965.

LOCAL HISTORY

One Hundred Years. The Story of Christ Church, Forest Hill, by the
Rev. R. P. Wernham, MBE. Thanet Press, Margate, 1954.

MALTA

British Malta, by A. V. Laferla. Malta Government Printing Office,
1938.

Malta, by Sir Harry Luke, KCMG. Harrap, 1949.

MEDICAL HISTORY

The History of Bacteriology, by William Bulloch, MD, FRS. OUP,
1938.

King's and Some King's Men, by H. Willoughby Lyle, MD, FRCS.
OUP, 1935/50.

The First Anaesthetic: the Story of Crawford Long, by Frank Kells Boland, MD. University of Georgia Press, Athens, 1950.

A History of Medicine, by Douglas Guthrie, MD, FRCS.Ed, FRSE. Nelson, 1958.

A Short History of Medicine, by Charles Singer, MD, revised by E. A. Underwood. Clarendon Press, 1962.

The Development of Modern Surgery from 1830, by Frederick F. Cartwright, LRCP, MRCS, FFARCS. Arthur Barker, 1967.

THE CRIMEA

Letters from the Black Sea, during the Crimean War 1854–5, by Admiral Sir Leopold George Heath, KCB. Richard Bentley and Son, 1897.

Memories of the Crimean War, January 1855 to June 1856, by Douglas Arthur Reid, MD. St Catherine's Press, 1911.

The Destruction of Lord Raglan, by Christopher Hibbert. Longmans, 1961.

Battles of the Crimean War, by W. Baring Pemberton. Batsford, 1962.

GENERAL AND MILITARY HISTORY

Notes on Matters affecting the Health, Efficiency and Hospital Administration of the British Army, by Florence Nightingale. Harrison, 1858.

Roll of Commissioned Officers in the Medical Service of the British Army 1727–1898, by Charles William Johnston, CB, MA, MD. Aberdeen, at the University Press, 1917.

The History of England, by Sir Charles Oman, KBE. Arnold, 1926.

The Royal Army Service Corps, by John Fortescue. CUP, 1930.

Not Least in the Crusade. A Short History of the Royal Army Medical Corps, by Peter Lovegrove. Gale and Polden, 1951.

Index

This Index is divided into two main sections – *General Subjects* and *Personalities*: each of these being further subdivided as shown. References to Illustrations are printed in *italics: fp* = facing page.

GENERAL SUBJECTS

PERSONALITIES